The Young Reader's Shakespeare
ROMEO & JULIET

A Retelling by Adam McKeown

Illustrated by Peter Fiore

STERLING PUBLISHING CO., INC.

NEW YORK

Library of Congress Cataloging-in-Publication Data

McKeown, Adam (Adam N.)
   Romeo & Juliet : young reader's Shakespeare /
adapted for prose by Adam McKeown.
      p. cm.
   Includes index.
   Summary: A prose retelling of William
Shakespeare's play about two young people who fall
in love despite their families' age-old feud. Includes
background information, character summary, and
commonly asked questions.
   ISBN 1-4027-0004-0
   1. Romeo (Fictitious character)—Juvenile
fiction. 2. Juliet (Fictitious character)—Juvenile
fiction. 3. Verona (Italy)—Juvenile fiction.
4. Vendetta—Juvenile fiction. [1. Shakespeare,
William, 1564–1616—Adaptations.] I. Shakespeare,
William, 1564–1616. Romeo and Juliet. II. Title.
  PR2878.R6M37 2003
  822.3'3–dc21   2003006162

Book design by Deborah Kerner/
Dancing Bears Design

2 4 6 8 10 9 7 5 3 1

Published by Sterling Publishing Co., Inc.
387 Park Avenue South, New York, NY 10016
Text © 2004 by Adam McKeown
Illustrations © 2004 by Peter Fiore
Distributed in Canada by Sterling Publishing
c/o Canadian Manda Group,
One Atlantic Avenue, Suite 105
Toronto, Ontario, Canada M6K 3E7
Distributed in Great Britain and Europe by Chris
Lloyd at Orca Book Services, Stanley House, Fleets
Lane, Poole BH 15 3AJ, England
Distributed in Australia by Capricorn Link
(Australia) Pty. Ltd.
P.O. Box 704, Windsor, NSW 2756, Australia

Sterling ISBN 1-4027-0004-0

Contents

About Shakespeare and Romeo and Juliet

Shakespeare is the most celebrated writer in the history of the English language, and yet we know very little about him. He was born in 1564, in a town called Stratford-upon-Avon. Shakespeare's career as a playwright and actor began in London in the early 1590s, when he was in his late twenties. He wrote more than thirty plays as well as many poems in the space of about twenty years. Scholars believe his last play was performed sometime around 1611, just five years before he died.

Mostly from church and legal records, we are able to piece together a partial story of Shakespeare's life. He married a woman named Anne Hathaway when he was eighteen or so and had three children. We have no record that Shakespeare ever attended school, but we suppose he did—and from his writing we can see that he knew most of the books of poetry, manners, and history that literate people of his time would have read. Nevertheless, he was criticized by some for his lack of education. At a time when a well-educated person would have been completely fluent in Latin and familiar with ancient Greek, Shakespeare, apparently, was fluent in neither. Yet, his Latin was probably better than almost anyone's today.

The main reason we know so little about Shakespeare is that in the sixteenth century, theater was considered popular entertainment, not high art. Like television programs today, plays back then were often the product of many writers working together, and some were not attributed to any author at all. Shakespeare, as far as we know, did not supervise the publication of any of his plays. The first published collection of his work did not appear until 1623, seven years after his death. Even though he was a well-known playwright and a successful theater manager, he was thought of as a "player," not as an important artist, so while people flocked to his plays, nobody paid much attention to his life.

How, from these beginnings, Shakespeare became the most famous writer in the history of the English-speaking world has been a matter much debated by scholars. However it happened, there is little disagreement now that Shakespeare's talent soars above everyone else's. Shakespeare has been described as "our Homer." Like the ancient Greek poet Homer, he seems able to sum up and give meaning to our civilization, our history, and ourselves. The real Shakespeare probably lies somewhere between the visionary poet and the lowly player. This series of books was created with an eye toward giving you a chance to think about both ideas of Shakespeare. Sometimes he does seem like a visionary poet. But at other times he seems to be just like any of us—an ordinary person with ordinary concerns about children, law and order, money, and the future. Part of the fun of reading Shakespeare is seeing how he is both a man of almost superhuman intellect and a man who could live across the street.

The book you are about to read is based on a play that has become one of the most famous love stories ever written. Yet *Romeo and Juliet* is much more than a love story. Written early in Shakespeare's career (perhaps in 1594), it deals with a broad range of issues affecting young people—how to balance the expectations of parents with one's own desires, how to manage emotions, how to negotiate the problems created by older generations, and how to reconcile ideals to the practical demands of everyday life. *Romeo and Juliet*, however, is admired as much for the beauty of its language as for the issues it raises. For this reason, I have tried to leave as much of Shakespeare's language intact as I could. That said, any adaptation of a play, which is meant to be seen, into a story meant to be read, requires the addition of description—especially with Shakespeare's plays, which contain very few stage directions.

Romeo and Juliet poses the additional problem of being somewhat "raw" by Shakespeare's standards. Many of the characters and scenes are not as carefully developed as their counterparts in his more mature work. In order to make this version of *Romeo and Juliet* as rich and coherent as possible, I drew heavily on different stage and film productions I have seen, and equally on the imaginations of my colleagues and students. The nice thing—and also the frustrating thing—about *Romeo and Juliet* is that it leaves plenty of room for the reader's own interpretation. Even the basic personalities of Romeo and Juliet are seen differently by different readers.

Someday soon, when you are reading Shakespeare's *Romeo and Juliet* for yourself, I hope you will think back to this version to see how your interpretations are different from mine. It is the perspective that each new reader brings to Shakespeare that allows his plays to speak to the world in which we live.

Chapter One

"I'll keep the peace, all right," said Sampson, "but I won't put up with their insults. If we see any Montagues, they'd best keep quiet."

"Or what?" asked Gregory.

"I'll kill them all."

"All?" Gregory stopped walking and looked at his friend, trying to shield his eyes from the blazing sun. It was morning, but it was already a hot day, too hot for angry words.

"Every one of them," said Sampson. "If they are Montagues, then I'll fight with them—if they say anything to me."

They began to walk on toward the square. "What if a dog from the house of Montague barks at you?" Gregory asked, half in jest.

"Then I'd fight with it."

"What about women?"

This time Sampson stopped, as if he had to think about the question. "It's all the same. Men, women—if they are Montagues, they are my enemies and will feel my anger."

"So you'd fight with the women?"

"I didn't say that," Sampson explained. "I said they'd feel my anger. I'd fight with the men and, having beaten them, be civil with the women."

"Be civil?"

"Yes."

"You mean you'd woo them? Once the Montague men were out of the way?"

"Yes, I suppose."

"But that's not really showing them your anger—unless you think wooing the women is the same as fighting with the men."

"Isn't it?" Sampson answered sharply. "Either way it's about showing the Montagues who's in charge. I'll conquer the men with clubs and swords, the women with smiles and pretty words. It's all the same."

"I wish it were," said Gregory, seeing two Montague manservants approaching from the other side of the square. "Then you could just smile and say kind things to these two and be satisfied."

As Sampson watched the men strut across the square, his face contracted into a scowl. "I can think of nothing kind to say."

Gregory grabbed the cuff of Sampson's jacket and gave it a jerk, discreetly but forcefully. "Then say nothing," he whispered. "Remember, we are not allowed to start trouble."

The two men angled towards Sampson and Gregory, looking at them with cold disdain, exchanging quiet remarks of an obviously nasty kind.

Gregory smiled unnaturally as the two passed by. Sampson did likewise, but he could not suppress his contempt. The men had not gone two paces when he put his thumb to his nose, stuck out his tongue, and went, "Thhhhhhhhhpppt!"

The men stopped and turned. "Do you thumb your nose at me, sir?" said one of them.

"Uh," whispered Sampson to Gregory, "is the law on our side if I say 'yes'?"

"No."

"Then, no," declared Sampson.

"But I saw you thumb your nose," said the man.

"And I heard you make a noise," said the other.

"Then I thumb my nose, sir," said Sampson innocently, "and I make a noise. What of it?"

"That's just like a man of the house of Capulet, isn't it, Abraham?" said the other man, nudging his companion. "Making rude gestures to honest people minding their own business. And too cowardly to own up to it."

"Just like a Capulet," Abraham agreed. "Cowards. Every one of them." He glared at Gregory. "And everyone who works for them."

"There's no reason to call anyone a coward," said Gregory.

"Right," Abraham laughed. "Why bother calling a man a coward when it is obvious that he is one?"

"I'll show you a coward!" said Sampson. He went for his dagger, but in so doing he jostled Gregory, who lurched forward into Abraham.

Abraham shoved Gregory back, yelling to his friend, "You saw that, Balthasar? You saw that? He came at me first!"

"I saw it," Balthasar said, and pulled a stiletto from his sash.

Gregory knew it was too late to keep the peace. It was every man for himself. He saw Sampson dash out and slice a gaping hole in Abraham's jacket.

With no further hesitation, Gregory rammed the butt of his walking stick into Balthasar's ribs, doubling him over. Then he swung wildly and landed a ferocious blow on Abraham's head. Abraham went down, just as Balthasar stuck his dagger into Gregory's leg.

"Ahhhhhh!" Gregory howled as he fell.

Sampson, fearing for his friend's life, tackled Balthasar before he had a chance to stab Gregory again. Then all four men wrestled in the dusty street. A crowd gathered around them, shouting and cheering.

Benvolio heard the commotion from his seat at an inn across the square, where he had been enjoying a peaceful breakfast. Though nephew to Old Montague himself, Benvolio did not think much of the ancient feud between his family and the Capulets. When he was a boy, he had not questioned it. When he was a teenager, he had even come to enjoy the danger of it.

But now that he was a man, although he was still young, he was tired of it all and recognized that hatred would only result in death, and death in more hatred. But the only way to break the cycle was to jump in between angry men and their swords. It was nothing he wanted to do, but something he knew he must. With that thought, he leapt to his feet and charged toward the fray.

"Peace! Put up your weapons!" Benvolio yelled, rushing in with his own sword drawn, pulling the men off each other.

As he did so, a hush fell over the crowd.

A tall, lean fellow strode forward, a cape flung over his shoulder. He slid his rapier from its sheath and touched a finger to its point.

"Just like a Montague," he sneered, "fighting alongside men of this kind. Turn and meet your death, Benvolio."

It was Tybalt, Capulet's nephew, an arrogant man of thirty whose vanity, petulance, and, unfortunately for Benvolio, swordsmanship were unmatched by anyone in Verona.

"Tybalt," said Benvolio. "Put away your sword. I'm trying to keep the peace. Now, help me part these men."

"Peace? You stand there with your sword drawn talking of peace? I hate the word," Tybalt spoke in a low voice around a twisted smile, "as I hate hell, all Montagues, and thee."

Benvolio scarcely had time to lift his blade in defense before Tybalt lunged at him.

The crowd cheered again. "Kill the Montagues!" some yelled. "Kill the Capulets!" yelled others. "Kill them all!" yelled more.

"Kill the Capulets?" muttered an old man in slippers, shuffling out of a church nearby.

It was Capulet, holding on to his young wife's arm. "My sword! Give me my sword!"

"A sword?" his wife scolded. "You need a cane, not a sword."

The ring of steel against steel filled the air. More and more people gathered around the fight, urging on the combatants.

"It's Capulet! I know it's Capulet." Another old man hobbled across the square. This time it was Montague. "Lead me over to him, I say!"

"How will you fight? You can barely walk!" said Lady Montague.

Benvolio struck Tybalt below the shoulder, but lightly—the blade only cut the fabric of his shirt. Tybalt spun around and jabbed, missing Benvolio's throat by a whisker.

Then the crowd went silent again as hoofbeats neared.

Benvolio looked up, panting. Tybalt lowered his sword.

Towards them rode Escalus, the prince of Verona, surrounded by his soldiers.

He circled Tybalt and Benvolio, glowering at both. The onlookers scurried away.

"Rebellious subjects!" roared the prince. "Enemies to peace! Throw your weapons to the ground!"

Tybalt and Benvolio did as the prince commanded.

"Now," Escalus said, "where are the responsible parties? And I don't mean you young hotheads but those two doddering graybeards whom you call your uncle and master. Whenever the quiet of my streets is disturbed, I know they are lurking close by." He searched the crowd and, sure enough, found the two old men. "You, Capulet, and you, Montague, come forward and stand before me."

The two old men shuffled forward and bowed their heads.

"You two are foremost among the men of this city and as such are supposed to be models of public virtue. But instead of showing my citizens how to live nobly, you have forced them to take sides in your pointless argument—an argument begun before anyone else here was even born. Well, I have been patient too long." He drew his sword. "Hear my words. If ever your squabble disturbs the streets again, your lives shall pay for it. Is that clear?"

Montague nodded. Capulet mumbled.

"Capulet," the prince continued, "you will come with me. Montague, you will come this afternoon." He stared at Benvolio and Tybalt, at Gregory and Sampson, and at Abraham and Balthasar. "The rest of you—go home. Now!"

Chapter Two

Montague's servants, Abraham and Balthasar, helped their master up the hill to his palace overlooking the fountains by the city gates. Lady Montague remained a few steps behind, talking to Benvolio.

"My Romeo was not in this fight, was he?"

"No, madam," said Benvolio. "And I swear I tried to make sure there was no fight at all. Tybalt—"

"I know," Lady Montague said. "The Capulets. They simply can't be reasoned with. They're beasts, absolute beasts. But no more of that. If Romeo wasn't with you, then where is he?"

"The last I saw him, madam, was this morning, just before daybreak. He was lying on the garden wall, sighing so mournfully I'd have thought the stones themselves would weep."

13

"Oh, my poor Romeo." Lady Montague wrung her hands. "Do you know the cause?"

"No, madam. I went to him, but he fled at my approach."

"I confess I have seen him often in the garden and asked what troubles him, but he says nothing to me." Lady Montague smiled sadly. "I had hoped he might have told you."

As they reached the steps of the Montague palace, a young man stepped out of the rows of eglantine.

Benvolio leaned in toward Lady Montague. "There's Romeo, now, madam, unless I'm mistaken. I'll talk to him again."

"If you please," said the lady, "though I fear he has told us all he intends to." She patted Benvolio's wrist and followed her husband up the steps.

"Good morning, cousin," Benvolio said to Romeo as he approached.

"Is it still morning?" said Romeo, tossing a stone into the pool in the center of the garden. "It has just struck nine."

"Sad hours pass slowly." Romeo threw another stone, more violently this time.

"What has made your hours seem so long?"

"Not having that which makes them short."

"You must mean love," said Benvolio merrily. "I suspected you were in love!"

Romeo threw a whole handful of stones into the fountain and then glowered as if he were daring the water to throw them back. "Out."

Benvolio wasn't sure what his cousin meant. Was he telling him to go? "I don't understand you, Romeo."

"Out," he repeated. "Not in love, but out of love. The one I love does not love me, so therefore I am out of love."

Benvolio chuckled at what he thought was a joke.

Evidently, Romeo had not been joking. "Do you laugh at me?" He turned and stared hard at Benvolio.

"No, no," Benvolio said, frightened for a moment by the intensity of Romeo's reaction. "It's just that—"

Romeo raised his hand. "Forgive me," he said, taking a deep breath. "I haven't slept in days—haven't been able to escape my own thoughts." As he spoke, he noticed the blood on Benvolio's face. "So much so that I didn't even see that my favorite cousin has been wounded."

"It's nothing," said Benvolio. "Just the usual scuffle with the Capulets. The blood isn't mine—I hope."

"I should have been there with you. Even if I couldn't have helped you, perhaps one of the Capulets might have run me through and put me out of my misery."

"You don't mean that." But something in Romeo's eyes suggested that he did. "You would rather die than be in love with someone who doesn't love you back?"

"I wish it were not so, but . . .," he kicked a stone loose and hurled it angrily into the water, "but little I have wished for lately has come true, so it doesn't matter what I wish."

"I hate to see you like this."

"Hate?" Romeo erupted, grabbing Benvolio by the shoulders. "Hate to see me in love? Then you hate me, for there is no other Romeo but the one in love!" He shook his cousin. "But maybe you would rather love to see me in hate? Is that it? Perhaps that would make more sense to you. Montagues love to hate, after all, love to fight and kill. But don't you see that whether we love to hate or love to love doesn't matter? It's the same passion—the same excess of passion, and it will kill us just the same. Leave me to my love, if you hate to see me, and I will leave you to your hate."

Romeo's words did not sit well with Benvolio, who, after all, had just risked his life to stop a fight earlier that morning, but he knew Romeo was nearly at his wits' end. He also knew Romeo was correct to identify the problem with his family as one of excessive passion. Benvolio did not say, for fear of upsetting his cousin further, that Romeo himself suffered more from that problem than anyone else in the family. He had known Romeo since boyhood and had never met anyone so prone to violent mood swings, capable of being as elated one moment as he was dejected the next. Now, however, was not the time to discuss that problem. He wanted to help his cousin in any way he could. He spoke slowly and softly to convey calm.

"Can you at least say who it is that has put you in this state? Who are you in love with? Tell me."

Romeo released his grasp on Benvolio. "A woman," he mumbled.

"Yes," said Benvolio. "Who?"

"Rosaline," said Romeo. The sound of the word seemed to crush his soul. "Rosaline."

"Rosaline?" Benvolio brightened. "If it is the Rosaline I'm thinking of, then all is not lost. I happen to know that tonight, this very night, she will be at a party in Capulet's house."

Romeo did not stir. "In Capulet's house? My father's enemy? I might as well go straight to my grave since I would surely be killed if I entered the house of Capulet. Though perhaps that wouldn't be so bad. . . ."

"Cousin," said Benvolio. "Mercutio, the prince's kinsman and our friend, is also an invited guest. We can go with him—masked. No one will recognize us."

Romeo looked up.

"Not ready to die yet, eh?" Benvolio was happy to see his cousin's spirits rise, if only a little. "But I warn you, there will be so many beautiful ladies there, you'll probably forget all about Rosaline."

"Heresy, Benvolio. You profane her name and mine to say there is anyone more beautiful than she or that I would forsake her for another."

"Believe what you want," said Benvolio, helping Romeo to his feet. "Just get yourself ready for that party. One way or another it will be good for you."

Chapter Three

Capulet leaned back in his chair as Paris, the prince's young kinsman, brought him a cup of cool water.

"Thank you, my boy," said Capulet, taking a sip. "As I was saying, the good thing is that Montague is bound to the same decree that I am. Both of us will die if either of us breaks the peace. Heh." He laughed. "Break the peace. That's funny."

"How so?" asked Paris.

"Because the two of us can barely break bread these days, let alone break the peace. Men as old as we are should be able to stay out of a fight."

"You may, sir, and so may Montague, but what about your young kinsmen? They aren't always clearheaded when their passions are aroused."

"Oh," said Capulet, "the young think with their hearts and not their heads—they always will—but they will listen to their elders and follow our example."

"Let us hope so," said Paris. "And you are both such noble gentlemen. It's a pity this quarrel has gone on so long."

"And to tell the truth, I think I've forgotten how it started." Capulet laughed again.

Paris laughed with him, but he was eager to change the subject. "Have you had a chance to give some more thought to my request?"

"Your request? I had almost forgotten that too." Capulet didn't laugh this time.

"You are opposed to the marriage then?" asked Paris.

"No," Capulet answered, "though I can't say I'm altogether for it. Not that you aren't a good man—you're one of the finest I know. And a father could do worse than having the prince's nephew for a son-in-law. But Juliet is so young. Give her two more years."

"Many ladies younger than she are already mothers," Paris gently objected.

"Because they are too soon married!" snapped Capulet. But he knew the young man was right. Capulet's own wife was Juliet's age when he married her—and Paris was much closer to that age than he had been. There was no reason Juliet couldn't marry Paris. But Capulet just wasn't ready to see his only daughter all grown up, married, and with a family of her own. It made him feel old. But he *was* old, he reminded himself, and Juliet *was* all grown up. If he cared about her so much, why wouldn't he want her to marry, to start a life of her own with a good man? After all, she couldn't stay his little girl forever.

"I'm afraid I've upset you," said Paris, rising to leave. "Perhaps I have pressed the issue too hard. You are her father, and you know what is best for her."

"Wait," said Capulet.

Paris stopped.

"I'll give you my consent." He raised his hand. "But the decision is hers. There will be a party here tonight. Come. If you can win her heart, then you will have my blessing."

"I will!" cried Paris. "Thank you, I will!"

"Send in my servant so I can pass the news along to her mother."

Paris did as he was told and left.

Alone, Capulet sank back into his chair. He looked out through his window at the gum trees waving in the breeze. The sun warmed his face and the sound of the wind through the leaves soothed him. He let himself imagine Juliet falling in love and in doing so he remembered falling in love himself.

And he went to sleep.

Chapter Four

"Nurse!" Lady Capulet crossed her arms and tapped her foot against the marble floor of the hall. "Nurse!"

"Coming, madam," came a voice from above.

The nurse tramped down the steps, huffing and puffing, her florid face shiny with perspiration. "Here, madam." She collapsed onto a stool and began to fan herself with her apron.

"Where's my daughter?" demanded Lady Capulet.

"I told her to come."

"Well, tell her again."

"My la-amb!" the nurse shouted up the stairs. "My ladybird! Where are you, Juliet!"

"I could have done that," hissed Lady Capulet.

"Who calls?" came another voice.

"Your mother," shouted the nurse.

Juliet appeared at the balustrade, her long black hair spilling out from beneath a silver headband. She held a colorful Book of Hours in her small white hands. "Here, Mother," she said demurely.

"Nurse," Lady Capulet snapped her fingers, "leave us a while. We must talk in secret."

"Talk in secret?" the nurse said, moping toward the kitchen. "Don't trust me with secrets. I only raised her since she was in diapers."

Lady Capulet ignored the nurse and met her daughter's keen, dark eyes.

Somehow, when no one was looking, Juliet had become a woman, and Lady Capulet wasn't comfortable with the idea. It had been hard enough for her to get to know the child, and now she had to start all over again with a grown woman who had a mind and a will all her own. She wasn't sure if she had the patience or, really, the desire to do it.

"Secrets, madam?" Juliet said in an uninviting tone. The last thing she wanted to talk about with her mother was anything secret. Her mother just didn't know how to deal with anything private or intimate. She would either express concern or, worse, offer some stupid and embarrassing advice. For this reason, whenever her mother cornered her, seeking serious conversation, Juliet made it as difficult as possible.

Lady Capulet looked at the little slit of a smile on Juliet's face. It had once been so innocent, that smile, and now it always seemed—she wasn't sure even how to describe it—not scheming exactly, but willful, definitely willful. As she tried to imagine talking about marriage with a girl who wouldn't listen to her and would only speak in one-word answers, she felt suddenly exhausted.

"Nurse," she commanded, "come back again! You should hear this, too."

The nurse ran in, grinning from ear to ear. "I love secrets!"

"Now," began Lady Capulet stiffly, "you know, my daughter, you are, as they say, 'of age.'"

"You don't have to tell me, madam," replied the nurse. "Look at her, will you? She's already almost as tall as you are, madam, and fills out a dress as well, too."

"Indeed," Lady Capulet agreed coldly.

"But I miss those days, I do. She was the prettiest baby I ever held." The nurse smiled at Juliet. "And you still are. If I might live to see you married, I'd have my wish."

"Marriage." Lady Capulet clapped her hands together, happy that the nurse had broached the subject she was having difficulty coming around to. "That is exactly what I want to talk about. Tell me, Juliet, how would you like to be married?"

The question was awkward. It sounded to Juliet as though her mother were asking about marriage in general, but that was unlike her. Was her mother really about to ask if she wanted to be married, Juliet wondered. Of course, she always imagined that someday she would be married, but not anytime soon. Still, it was best, she knew, not to defy her mother openly, so she chose her words carefully before making a reply. "It is an honor I dream not of," she said politely. "I am too young to think of marriage."

"Well, think of it now. I was a mother at about the same age you are now."

"Many times you have told me," replied Juliet, less politely than before.

Lady Capulet let out a breath. She was tired of talking, and she could see that Juliet was not going to make this difficult discussion easy. "I will be brief. The valiant Paris seeks you for his wife."

"Paris!" squawked the nurse. "That's a man anyone would marry! Paris? Oh, my ladybird, Paris wants you for his wife!"

"What do you say, Juliet? Can you love the gentleman? He'll be at the party tonight. You may take a good look at him before you answer."

"Ooo! I'll help you with that!" the nurse burst out. "I like looking over pretty gentlemen."

Lady Capulet closed her eyes and waited for the nurse's laughter to stop. "Speak briefly, daughter. Can you love Paris?"

"I will look to like," Juliet said mechanically, "if looking liking move."

Is that a yes? Lady Capulet wondered. She was about to ask but wasn't sure if she wanted the answer. "Be happy you have the choice," she said. "When I was your age, ladies loved according to their parents' will, not according to their own."

"As you have also told me often," said Juliet. "And of course your will is my own, Mother."

"Of course, daughter," said Lady Capulet.

Chapter Five

"Come on, come on!" Mercutio yelled to Romeo and Benvolio. "We're burning daylight!"

"Daylight's already spent!" came an angry voice from a second story window nearby. "Hold your peace or I'll call the constable!"

"It is a figure of speech, sir," Mercutio yelled back in mock civility. "I mean, sir, we delay."

The shutters closed with a slam.

Mercutio made a rude noise. "I would have thought a lover would have flown here on Cupid's wings," Mercutio jeered as Romeo and Benvolio approached. "What has taken you two so long?"

"You are wrong, Mercutio," Romeo said. "Love's burden is heavy, and so a lover's feet are slow."

"And does that mean you will not dance tonight, you heavy-footed lover?" Mercutio did a two-step. "If I were a lover, I would surely dance."

"What do you know about love?" Benvolio asked, coming to his cousin's rescue.

"I know that lovers are possessed," answered Mercutio.

"Possessed?" said Benvolio. "By what?"

"Not by what, but by whom," said Mercutio.

"Then by whom?" demanded Benvolio.

Mercutio dropped his voice into a whisper as if he were revealing something forbidden and dangerous. "By Queen Mab, of course."

"Queen Mab?" said Benvolio.

"Shhhhh!" Mercutio put his finger to his lips. "You don't want to call her name. She might come."

"There is no Queen Mab," said Romeo.

"There is," insisted Mercutio.

"Well, I've never seen her."

"You wouldn't," Mercutio said. "She comes in a shape no bigger than an agate stone on an alderman's ring. Her chariot is an empty hazelnut made by a squirrel—its wheel spokes are spider's legs. Dressed in moonshine, she gallops through the night, riding into people's noses as they lie asleep. She makes soldiers dream of swords, merchants of money, courtiers of curtsies, and . . ." he paused and pointed a finger at Romeo, ". . . lovers of love."

"Enough, Mercutio. You're talking about nothing," Romeo said.

"True," Mercutio answered, "I'm talking of dreams, which are the children of an idle brain, nothing but vain fantasy, as inconstant as the wind."

"All your wind is blowing us off course," laughed Benvolio. "I'm sure supper's already ended, and we'll likely miss the dance if we stand here listening to you any longer."

"It's just as well," said Romeo. "I fear this night will end in disaster."

"Just for that," said Mercutio, "I'm going to shut up and hurry along. I wouldn't want to keep a lover from his appointed disaster. Come on!"

He sped down the darkened street. Benvolio and Romeo followed.

They arrived at a gate that led into a quiet garden, beyond which a door to the great hall stood open. They could see within a golden light and hear the muffled sounds of music and merriment.

"I suggest you assume your disguises," said Mercutio. "Otherwise, the doorman will never let you in, filthy Montagues such as you are."

They made their way through the garden and stopped at the door to the hall, which was guarded by one of Capulet's servants. Within, drummers kept time on their tabors as the oboes played. The ladies danced to the music, their veils fluttering behind them like the wings of birds. The men followed their movements, touching only the hands of the ladies, and then only on the heavy drumbeats that marked the end of each measure. The torches hanging from the square beams of the ceiling cast strange shadows on the floor as the dancers glided to the slow cadence of the music.

"There are three maskers here," the doorman called out, as Mercutio, Benvolio, and Romeo stepped forward.

"Maskers! Well, let them in, let them in," cried Capulet, teetering over to the door just as the music came to an end. "Welcome, gentlemen. It's been a long time since I've put on a mask and whispered into a fair lady's ear, but I have a mind to join you."

Capulet's old cousin came up beside him. "You? Dance alongside these young maskers? You'll trip them up and get in their way."

Capulet laughed. "Very likely. How long has it been since you and I last went to a party masked?"

"Too long, cousin."

"Not so long!"

"Since before your wife was even a sparkle in her mother's eye, and look—your wife's child is now out on the dance floor. A few more sparkles in her eye and you two will be grandparents. You are old, cousin. Admit it."

Lady Capulet, who was standing nearby, smiled painfully at the thought of being a grandparent.

"Well," said Capulet, "I suppose you and I are past our dancing days. Let's give the floor to the younger folks. Make room in the hall for three more!"

The music started again. Mercutio and Benvolio joined the dance, while Romeo mingled instead among the crowd of onlookers, hoping to see his beloved Rosaline.

But he saw someone else.

She seemed like a picture or a reflection in a magic glass. She moved effortlessly as if her feet were not anchored to the earth or as if she were composed of pure air. No, Romeo thought, not pure air but pure fire. Something burned in her, something beyond beauty. A rare power. A force. She was a spirit—an angel, but not an angel as we imagine them.

"Oh, she teaches the torches to burn bright," Romeo murmured to himself. "It seems she hangs upon the cheek of night as a rich jewel in an Ethiopian's ear."

He walked forward as if in a trance. Did my heart love till now? he asked himself. "No," he said aloud in answer. "No, my eyes have lied, for I never saw true beauty till this night."

He lifted his mask, hoping the lady would see his face. She did.

"What troubles you, fair lady?" asked Paris, as Juliet stopped dancing suddenly as if she had been hit by a dart.

"Nothing," she answered. "Something in my eye."

They danced on, but Juliet could not take her eyes off the face she had seen at the edge of the floor.

Neither could her cousin. I know that face, Tybalt thought. Is that the fellow I met last week at tennis? No, that wasn't it, but who? He seems like a fine gentleman— someone worthy of my company.

"Boy!" he barked to his servant. "That young gentlemen there. Go and ask his name and tell him that Tybalt, heir of the house of Capulet, would like to grace him with . . ."

As he studied the face he slowly remembered where he had seen it before.

In the square.

Tybalt began to seethe.

"Grace him with, uh, what, sir?" the servant asked nervously.

"My sword," Tybalt growled through clenched teeth. "Get me my sword."

The servant gulped and did as he was told.

"A Montague!" Tybalt punched his hand. "Come to our party, masked. To mock us!"

"What's the matter?" asked Capulet coming over to Tybalt. "What's gotten you out of sorts?"

"Uncle," said Tybalt, pointing to Romeo, "this is a Montague."

Capulet peered across the dance floor. "Young Romeo, is it?"

"Romeo," Tybalt said. "That villain!"

"Calm down, nephew," Capulet said, placing his hand on Tybalt's shoulder. "Leave him alone. He bears himself like a good gentleman, as all Verona claims him to be." Capulet patted his headstrong nephew. "Be patient. Take no note of him."

"Too late," returned Tybalt, shaking free of his uncle's hand.

Capulet didn't like the young man's insolence, but he checked his irritation and continued to reason with him.

"It is my will," he said, "and out of respect for me, if not for Romeo's reputation, put yourself in good cheer. Frowns do not belong at a party."

"Frowns belong at a party when such a villain is a guest. I'll not tolerate him."

"You'll not tolerate him?" Capulet scolded, "he shall be tolerated!"

Tybalt turned his back on his uncle.

"How dare you, boy!" thundered Capulet, clutching Tybalt by the elbow and spinning him around. "Am I the master here or you? I say he shall be left alone."

"It's a shame," muttered Tybalt.

"Is it so indeed?" Capulet said. "You're a saucy boy."

"I'm thirty years old," snapped Tybalt. "I'm not a boy!"

"And do you think you'll be a man by causing trouble among my guests?"

As their voices rose, the dancers became uneasy. The musicians stopped playing.

"Pardon, my lady," said Paris to Juliet. "Your family matters must now be mine, if I am to be your husband. I'll see what's the trouble."

"Of course," said Juliet, but she hadn't even heard what Paris said. He was leaving, and that was good.

Capulet saw that he and Tybalt were making a scene. "This is just a game we're playing. See?" he declared. "The boy must be contrary with me. You go now, rascal." He pinched Tybalt's cheek. "Make merry. The dance awaits."

Tybalt went along with the charade as the music started again. He smiled, tight-lipped, bowed to his uncle, and stepped away.

"Cousin?" said Paris to Tybalt, as he approached.

Tybalt pushed past him.

"Let him go," said Capulet. "He'll behave himself. I'm the master of this house."

Out on the floor, Juliet heard a whisper in her ear. "The dance is starting," it said. "But follow me and let it wait."

"Where shall it wait?" She turned and saw the face she had seen before. Even behind the mask, it was the most beautiful thing she had ever beheld.

She followed him to a private place beyond the glow of the torches and away from the commotion of the dance. Romeo removed his mask and took Juliet by the hand.

"If I profane with my unworthy hand this holy shrine," he said, "my two lips ready stand to smooth that rough touch with a tender kiss."

Juliet felt the blood rush into her cheeks, but she kept her poise. "You do wrong your hand too much," she said, "but if you call my hand a holy shrine, that would make me a saint. And shouldn't you pray before a saint?"

"Pray?" asked Romeo.

"Pray," said Juliet. And with that she gently laced her fingers through his, holding his hand tight, as if their two hands were locked in prayer.

Romeo shivered. The sensation of her hand touching his was almost too much to bear, but it was also frustrating. Now that he held her hand, he wanted more. He wanted to kiss her, and yet she had not given permission! He couldn't stand it. "Have not saints lips?" he said, stroking her thumb with his.

"Yes," she said. She knew what Romeo was getting at—and she wanted him to kiss her more than she had ever wanted anything—but she didn't wish to seem too bold. "But lips are also for praying."

"Oh, then, dear saint, let lips do what praying hands do. That is my prayer."

Juliet knew it wasn't proper for a young lady to tell a man whose name she didn't even know to go ahead and kiss her, but it was all she could think about. His touch was so warm, so strong, and so gentle that she could almost imagine what his lips would feel like pressing against her own. But how could she get him to do it? As Romeo looked at her, waiting for an answer, Juliet turned away for fear that her eyes would betray her desire.

"I see my prayer does not move you," said Romeo sadly. He began to release her hand.

But Juliet would not let go. "Saints do not move," she said, "even when they have answered prayers." She closed her eyes and guided Romeo's hand to her heart.

Romeo felt Juliet's heart pounding within her chest. Or was it his own pulse shaking his hand? He couldn't tell. She was so beautiful standing there, he could almost believe she was a saint, some divine creature too perfect to suffer a mortal's kiss. For one terrible moment he even thought that if he did kiss her he would melt away or burn up instantly, as if Juliet were the sun or a sacred flame in which the awesome power of all of the gods was manifest at once.

And, somehow, in a way Romeo neither tried to understand nor could have understood, it was this terror, this possibility of total annihilation, that drove him to do what he did next.

He kissed her.

"Madam!" bellowed the nurse, elbowing her way toward them. "Madam, your father and Paris are looking for you."

Juliet stepped away, still staring at Romeo.

Romeo slipped his mask back on. "Who is her father?"

The nurse had recognized the young Montague before he had a chance to put his mask back on.

"Why, this is Juliet, and her father, you should know, is the master of the house."

"She is a Capulet?"

"As you are a—"

"Bachelor!" interrupted Benvolio, hurrying towards Romeo. "Come," he whispered urgently. "We've been discovered. We need to get out of here before there's trouble."

"There already is trouble," said Romeo, as Benvolio whisked him away.

"Who . . . who was that gentleman?" Juliet asked.

"The handsomest I've ever laid eyes on," the nurse said.

"Will you . . . follow him and ask if he is married?" stammered Juliet.

"I can tell you now that he isn't, but might as well be."

Juliet just stared at the nurse, still entranced by the face she had seen, the hands she had touched, the lips she had kissed. "What do you mean?"

"His name is Romeo and he is a Montague, the only son of your great enemy."

"Of course, he would have to be a Montague," said Juliet.

"Huh?" the nurse said.

But Juliet did not bother to explain. Something about Romeo was impossible from the start, and she felt, even while kissing him, that either he was not real or that her whole sense of what was real would have to change because of him. As she repeated his name in her head, she saw her world dissolve and re-form into something else, something she could not yet hold in her imagination. As terrifying as it all was, she could no longer picture herself living in the old world, the one before Romeo, the one that had been all she had known until only a few minutes before. That Romeo was her enemy only made this feeling more intense, and she resolved at that moment that the world—and not her love—would have to change. It was as simple as that. "So," she said, "my only love sprung from my only hate."

"What's this? Love?" twittered the nurse. "My baby girl in love?"

"Juliet!" came a call from somewhere. It was Paris. Or her father. Juliet couldn't tell which and didn't care.

"Tell them I've gone to bed."

Chapter Six

"Romeo! My cousin Romeo!" Benvolio heard his own voice echo down the deserted street.

"He's gone to bed, and we should, too." Mercutio yawned.

"Why did he run away from us?"

"Who knows?"

"Aren't you worried about him?"

"No."

"Well, I am," said Benvolio. "Romeo!" he called again.

"Romeo!" Mercutio mocked. "Very well, if you want Romeo, we will flush him out, but you can't call a lover, you must conjure him. Like so." He cleared his throat and called, "Romeo! Appear in the likeness of a sigh. Recite one line of silly love poetry, and I'll know you're there! I conjure you by Rosaline's bright eyes, by her high forehead, and her scarlet lips." He grinned. "That should get him, if he's within earshot."

"That should get him angry, anyway."

"You're getting me angry!" shouted a man in a nightcap who had thrown open a shutter above them. "Get to bed!"

"Good man," said Mercutio, "might there be one forlorn lover there with you? He walks about the streets sighing, calling ladies' names to the empty night, what-have-you. One bed may be as good as another to a young man in his condition. Have you seen him?"

"I'm getting my club!" growled the man.

"Come," said Benvolio, pulling Mercutio by the arm. "I think you're right, after all. Romeo probably has gone home. And if he's wandering the streets, then, well, love is blind, as they say, and so he should be right at home in the dark. Let's leave him to it."

Strange thoughts filled Romeo's head. There was no going home. What would he do there? He wouldn't be able to sleep, and the thought of wandering around the garden all night seemed ridiculous. He wanted—no, he needed— to see Juliet again, but he could not go to her, not to her father's house.

And yet there was nowhere else to go.

He made his way through the night, back to the house of his father's enemy. There he climbed the garden wall and waited for he knew not what. As he crouched down low in the bushes, a terrible idea came to him: If I am found here I will die, but I would rather die here than live anywhere else. He breathed deeply and prepared himself for what might happen.

And yet he could not have prepared himself for what did happen.

From within a lonely upper room, a single candle blossomed in the darkness, casting the shadow of a woman upon the curtain.

"But soft," whispered Romeo, "what light through yonder window breaks?"

The door opened slowly and onto the balcony stepped Juliet.

"It is the east," gasped Romeo, "and Juliet is the sun! Arise, fair sun, and kill the envious moon, who is already sick and pale with grief, that you, her maid, are far more fair than she. It is my lady. Oh, it is my love! Oh, that she knew she were!"

Juliet carried the candle to the marble rail and stood beside it. She looked out into the darkness. Her lips parted.

"She speaks," whispered Romeo to himself, "but she says nothing. But there is language in her eyes, and I will answer it." He began to stand. "But I am too bold. It is not to me her eyes speak." He sank back down. "See how she leans her cheek upon her hand. Oh, that I were a glove upon that hand, that I might touch that cheek."

And then she spoke. "Ah, me!"

"Oh, speak again, bright angel," said Romeo softly.

He watched her shoulders rise and fall as she breathed. He wanted to run to

her, to climb the balcony, to comfort her, to do anything she asked. But wouldn't he then have to reveal his iden- tity, he thought, reveal himself as the son of her father's enemy? And then wouldn't she have to scorn him? He could not bear the thought. A burning lump rose in his throat.

Juliet spoke again: "Oh, Romeo, Romeo, wherefore art thou Romeo? Deny thy father and refuse thy name. Or, if you will not, be but sworn my love and I'll no longer be a Capulet."

Romeo's knees buckled. He fell backward. Had he died? Was this heaven? He stood and looked. Juliet was still there. It was all real. Should he say some- thing, he wondered. No. Not yet.

"It is but thy name that is my enemy," Juliet said. "What's a Montague?" She gestured impatiently. "It is not hand nor foot nor arm nor face nor any other part belonging to a man." She began to pace. "Oh, be some other name! What's in a name? A rose by any other word would smell as sweet. Romeo, doff your name, and for your name, which is no part of thee—take all myself."

Romeo couldn't stand it anymore. There she was—more beautiful than at the party—in her nightdress, with her hair undone.

"I take thee at thy word!" he cried, coming forward. "Call me but love, and I'll be new baptized. Henceforth, I never will be Romeo."

"What man are you, hidden in the night?" said Juliet, stepping back.

"I don't know how to tell you who I am," said Romeo. "My name is hateful to myself because it is an enemy to you."

"My ears have not yet drunk a hundred words from your tongue, yet I know the sound. Are you Romeo, and a Montague?"

"Neither, fair maid, if either you dislike."

Juliet smiled. Her breath came quickly. "How came you here? Tell me," she demanded, "and why? The orchard walls are high and hard to climb, and the place death, if any of my kinsmen find you here."

"With love's light wings did I leap over these walls, for stony barriers cannot hold love out. And love will try anything love can do." He held his hands up to her. "Your kinsmen are no stop to me."

Love? Romeo had said love. He had scaled the walls, risking certain death at the hands of Tybalt or her father, because of love—for her. She wanted him to say it again but she was afraid. "I would not for the world they saw you here."

"Let them find me," said Romeo. "My life were better ended by their hate than prolonged wanting your love."

She closed her eyes, but he still stood there in her imagination, even more perfect than in life, if such a thing were possible. "Do you love me?" she whispered.

"Lady, by yonder blessed moon I swear—"

"Oh, swear not by the moon—the inconstant moon—that changes monthly in her circled orb, lest your love prove likewise variable!"

"What shall I swear by?" Romeo asked.

"Don't swear at all," Juliet decided. "Or, if you will, swear by your gracious self." Her breaths were short and broken. "Swear by yourself and I will believe you."

"Madam!" came a voice from within the house. It was the nurse.

Juliet's eyes shot open. "A noise. Go, dear love!"

Romeo began to tiptoe back toward the trees, but Juliet could not bear the thought of him leaving. "No, stay!"

"Julie-e-et!" called the nurse again.

Romeo didn't know what to do. The blood was coursing through his body. He felt a pulsing in his temples and in his hands.

"Will you leave me so unsatisfied?" he asked.

Juliet leaned over the balcony. "What satisfaction can you have tonight?" she said.

"The exchange of your faithful vow for mine."

"I gave it to you before you asked," she said, "but I wish I had it back."

"Why would you wish that?"

"Only to be able to give it to you again." Juliet smiled. "My love is as boundless as the sea," she whispered, "and as deep. The more I give to you, the more I have."

"My lady!" shouted the nurse.

"In a minute!" Juliet yelled back. Then, to Romeo, she said, "Three words more and good night, indeed. If your love is honorable and your purpose marriage, send me word."

"I will," said Romeo.

"When?"

"Tomorrow," promised Romeo boldly. "I'll come myself."

"No," said Juliet, "it's too dangerous. I'll send my nurse to find you. When will you be ready?"

"By . . . by nine o'clock tomorrow."

"'Tis twenty years till then," she said, "but I will endure it. Go, now."

Romeo stepped away.

"Wait!" Juliet said again. She couldn't bear to see him go. "I have forgot why I did call you back."

"Let me stand here till you remember," said Romeo.

"But I love to see you there so much I will forget I am supposed to remember to tell you why I wanted you to stand there."

"And I'll still stay to have you still forget, forgetting any other home but this."

"It's almost morning; I would have you gone," Juliet said, "and yet no farther than a wanton's bird, who lets it hop a little from her hand and then, with a silken thread, plucks it back again."

"I would I were thy bird."

"Sweet, so would I." Juliet smiled. "But I would kill thee with much cherishing." She blew a kiss. "Good night, good night—parting is such sweet sorrow that I shall say good night till it be morrow."

He could almost feel her kiss touch his lips. "I will not sleep till then," he said, and disappeared into the garden.

"Juliet?" said the nurse, inching back the curtain and stepping out onto the balcony. "Are you there, sweetness?"

"Yes, I'm here," grumbled Juliet. "Alone."

Chapter Seven

Friar Lawrence plucked a bud from a twisted vine and rolled it in his fingers. The aroma wafted up to his nose on the fresh morning air.

"Ahh!" He breathed it in and smiled. The earth is a miraculous thing, he thought. The same soil in which we bury our dead gives birth to new flowers.

He tossed the bud to the ground and carefully wiped his fingers clean on his apron. And from those same sweet flowers come the deadliest poisons, for those who know how to extract them.

Withdrawing a pair of scissors from his pouch, the friar began to prune his vines, humming a sad-happy melody as he worked.

"Good morning, Father," came an urgent voice.

Friar Lawrence turned and saw Romeo. "My boy," he said, "what are you doing out in the world at this hour? If you were an old man like me, I would say you rose to tend your garden or watch the birds, but I've never known a young man to lift his head from the pillow so early." He smiled warmly. "Or has our Romeo not been in his bed tonight?"

"Not in my bed, no, but I got the sweetest rest anyway."

"God will pardon our sins." Friar Lawrence crossed himself. "Was it with Rosaline that you were, eh, resting without sleeping?"

"Rosaline? I have forgotten the name."

"That's good, my son, but then where have you been?"

"Feasting with my enemy!" Romeo exclaimed. "That's where I forgot all about Rosaline and learned what true love is."

Friar Lawrence rubbed his eyes. Romeo was speaking too fast. He gathered that the young man was trying to say that he was in love with someone else.

A pity. The morning was calm and perfect, and Friar Lawrence did not particularly want to deal with anyone's problems. Not yet anyway.

"Be plain, Romeo," he said. "No riddling confessions."

"I love the daughter of Capulet," said Romeo. "And she loves me. Our courtship was brief, but our love is eternal. We exchanged vows, Father. We have sworn ourselves to each other. Will you . . . no . . . no—you *must* marry us today."

"Marry you!" Friar Lawrence shook his head. "After all the tears you shed for Rosaline, only yesterday—now you say you are sworn to another? I see young men love with their eyes and not their hearts."

"Didn't you scold me for loving Rosaline?"

"I scolded you for doting on her."

"Didn't you tell me to bury my love?"

"But not to sprout another so soon. You are too passionate."

"What do we live by if not our passions?"

"By our reason," insisted Friar Lawrence. "By our passions we die."

"So praise me for being reasonable. I now understand that you were right about Rosaline. I wasn't in love with her—it was just a fancy. But Juliet is perfect, and it is only reasonable to love perfection. Don't you see? It isn't because of passion but because of reason that I love her. You must marry us."

Friar Lawrence looked out at the sun climbing into the sky, burning off the last lingering veil of morning fog. I am old, he thought, too old to have this argument with someone who isn't listening. But marry someone so young and so rash? Without consulting with the parents? And where were the parents? Had either Montague or Capulet taken their eyes off their stupid quarrel long enough to notice that their children weren't asleep in their beds last night—or that their children were grown up? Probably not. And all Verona suffers for their selfishness.

"Father?" asked Romeo impatiently.

The friar didn't answer. He saw his city stretching out beneath the glowing rays of the sun, and he made a decision. It might not be the most prudent one, he thought, it might not be the right one, but it will force a peace. And he wanted peace. Peace in his city. Peace in his garden. Peace in his heart.

"You have not persuaded me, Romeo," said Friar Lawrence at last, "but for one reason only I will assist you. This marriage might turn your households' hatred to pure love."

"Love," repeated Romeo. "It is pure love."

Friar Lawrence tucked his scissors into his pouch and led Romeo to the church.

43

Chapter Eight

"Where the devil is Romeo?" Mercutio leaned back against the cathedral steps that led down to the square. He yawned and covered his eyes with a handkerchief.

"You say he wasn't home when you got there?"

"No," answered Benvolio, who was pacing nearby, "but Tybalt has sent a letter for him. Romeo's man told me."

"A challenge?" asked Mercutio.

Benvolio kicked at a stone. "Romeo will answer it."

"Then Romeo will die," said Mercutio. "Tybalt fights as merrily as other men sing. He's a fop and prancing peacock, but he's a swordsman of the very first order."

Benvolio knew Mercutio was right, but Romeo was no coward and he was easily excited. If Tybalt challenged him, Romeo probably would answer—and then Romeo would be killed. Benvolio didn't want to think about it.

"Alas, poor Romeo, he is already dead!" intoned Mercutio. "Stabbed with a wench's eye—shot through the ear with a love song, the very pin of his heart cleft by Cupid's butt shaft—"

"I'd feel better if we knew where he was," Benvolio said, ignoring him.

"I'd feel better if I had left the party a little sooner." Mercutio lifted the handkerchief from his eyes. "But isn't that our doomed lover now?"

"Romeo!" cried Benvolio.

"Signior Romeo," chirped Mercutio in a high voice, waving his handkerchief like a lady. "*Bonjour*, sir. So nice to see you, especially after what you gave us last night."

"Why," Romeo said, "what did I give you?"

"The slip, sir, the slip! Don't you remember?"

"Forgive me, good Mercutio," Romeo said. "I had very important business. What were you so concerned about?"

"About a friend of ours," said Mercutio. "He ran away in the middle of the night. He's been so distraught lately over love that we thought maybe he'd thrown himself off some high tower or just faded away sighing."

"Peace," said Benvolio. "Have you seen the letter, Romeo?"

"Letter?"

"Yes," said Mercutio. "From the house of Capulet, your mortal enemy."

Romeo's eyes lit up. "From the house of Capulet! What did it say? When did it come?"

"This morning," said Benvolio. "I'm surprised the news pleases you so."

"Is it news?" asked Romeo. "I cannot remember a time before I loved as I do now. A thousand years have passed since I last heard her voice, or so it seems to me. Where is the letter? Do you have it?"

"What do you mean 'her voice'?" asked Benvolio, puzzled.

"He's delirious," said Mercutio. "And I must be, too." He rubbed his eyes. "Is that a ship coming across the square?"

They all looked up and saw Juliet's nurse trudging toward them, her white shawl billowing out behind her like a sail.

"Oh, I see," said Mercutio, loudly enough for the nurse to hear. "It's just a fat lady."

"'Fat lady'!" The nurse turned red and ran at Mercutio, brandishing her fan like a dagger. "You ill-mannered wretch, I'll—"

"Peace!" yelled Benvolio. "Peace, Mercutio. Peace, good lady. What can we do for you, madam?"

"Humph!" snorted the nurse. "I was looking for young Romeo here, but I'm sorry to find him in the company of a scoundrel."

"Take him away," chirped Mercutio. "A forlorn lover is tedious company, even to us scoundrels."

"What can I do for you, madam?" asked Romeo.

"I would have a private conference with you, sir," said the nurse.

They stepped aside.

"What saucy man was that?"

"A gentleman who loves to hear himself talk," Romeo replied, "and who will speak more in a minute than he will stand to listen to in a month."

"If he speaks anything more against me, I'll take him down. And if I cannot, I'll find those who will!"

"He'll take himself down," said Romeo. "He mocks himself bitterly and in secret ten times more than he mocks the world."

"That may be, but I'm sorry he's a friend of yours." The nurse studied Romeo. "My young lady told me all, and I have news from her for you, but before I say it I will tell you this: If you intend to lead her to a fool's paradise it would be a very gross kind of behavior. She's so young. If you deal falsely with her—"

"Deal falsely?" protested Romeo. "I cannot deal falsely with her. In Juliet I discovered a truth I could have only imagined. My heart, my mind, and my soul are all one and dedicated to her."

The nurse's suspicions drained away as she listened to Romeo. Of course, she knew all about the fickle passions of young men, but there was something different about Romeo. He seemed so . . . handsome. Was that it? The nurse looked into the dark pools of his eyes, at the smooth curve of his chin. If he wasn't any more sincere than other young men, he surely was more beautiful. And when such a beautiful man tells you something, you want to believe it.

Romeo interrupted her reverie. "Does that satisfy you, my dear nurse?"

She blushed. "Dear nurse? Go on!"

"My lady loves you, and she is my dear. What is dear to her is dear to me, dear nurse."

"Oh, dear Romeo," she said. "You're going to make my lady very happy."

Romeo smiled. "I intend to," he said. "I've already spoken with Friar Lawrence. Help her devise some means to come to his cell, and there we will be married."

"Married," said the nurse. "How beautiful."

"As soon as she arrives."

"Yes," she said, "as soon."

But the nurse just stood there, staring into Romeo's eyes. "Rosemary and Romeo," she cooed. "They both begin with the same letter, and both are so sweet."

Romeo took her hand. "Lady?"

"Where is my head?" said the nurse. "I will tell Juliet. We will come to Friar Lawrence's cell to marry you. As soon as we can!"

Chapter Nine

Juliet paced back and forth in her bedroom. *I sent her at nine o'clock,* she thought. *What time is it now? She is so, so slow!*

She sat on her bed but popped right up again.

The sun is almost overhead. From nine to twelve is almost three hours. Three hours! How long does it take to walk into the town square and walk back? If she had passions and youthful blood, she would be as swift in motion as a ball.

The door creaked open below, and heavy footsteps shook the stairs.

"O God, here she comes—she's coming!" cried Juliet.

She threw open her bedroom door. "Oh, honey nurse, what news?" she begged. "Have you met with him? Why do you look so sad?"

"Give me a moment," said the nurse as she reached the top of the stairs. "Can't you see I'm out of breath?"

"How are you out of breath when you have enough breath to tell me you're out of breath?" Juliet shook her. "Is the news good or bad? Tell me!"

"Well," said the nurse, "you have made a foolish choice."

Juliet turned pale.

The nurse pinched her cheek. "You chose to tell me his face was better than any man's, but you should have said his hands, his feet, his legs—his whole body—are better too." The nurse fell backward on the bed.

Juliet jumped on top of her. "This I know!" she snarled, gripping the nurse by the collar. "But what said he of our marriage?"

"He mentioned it."

"Oh, you torment me!" cried Juliet, her hair falling in her eyes. "Am I going to be married today or not?"

The nurse grinned. "Listen to you! You weren't so impatient to marry Paris. Why? What about this beautiful, charming, perfect young man has you so eager all of a sudden to be married?"

Juliet stood up and gathered herself. "I'm not eager," she said indignantly. "But, come—what says Romeo?"

"Do you have to go to confession today?"

"I doubt Romeo asked if I have to make confessions!" Juliet declared. "Enough of this chatter. I want to know his words. Give them to me."

"Good," teased the nurse. "If you only want his words, I can let you have those. Leave the rest of him to me." She laughed.

Juliet collapsed in a frustrated heap at the foot of the bed.

The nurse took pity on her. "There, there. I was only playing with you. A young woman about to get married can forgive an old lady for being a little jealous." She smiled.

"Married?" The word echoed in Juliet's head.

"You see, in order to make confessions you have to go to Friar Lawrence's cell, and there you will find a husband to make you a wife."

Juliet gasped.

"Now I see the blood rush into your cheeks," said the nurse. "Get you to church. You'll find the whole man there."

Juliet threw her arms around the nurse. "Honest nurse!" she cried. "Thank you! Thank you! Let's go right now."

51

Chapter Ten

Friar Lawrence poured water from a crystal vial onto his fingertips and dabbed them dry with a white linen cloth. "May this holy act bring blessings to us all," he said.

But he had to laugh at himself. What he really wanted to say was that he hoped God would understand why he was about to perform a marriage he didn't really believe in. No, that wasn't quite it either. God would understand. It was Montague and Capulet who would not. Maybe, he thought, maybe I should just pray to God those two old brawlers don't take their anger out on me when they find out I've married their children without their permission. But sometimes a sacrifice is necessary for the greater good.

He just hoped he wouldn't be the one sacrificed.

"Amen already," said Romeo, impatient with Friar Lawrence's lengthy silence.

Friar Lawrence scolded him gently. "Calm yourself, Romeo," he said. "Live and love moderately if you want either love or life to last long."

But he knew Romeo wasn't one to be calmed. And neither was Juliet. She was just as head-

strong as he. And there she was, running up the path. Too fast, he thought. All too fast. What we ought to do is throw cold water on these two, send them home, and make their parents come to church to beg forgiveness for their sins. He laughed at himself again. But you're not going to make Montague or Capulet do anything, you tired old coward.

"Good afternoon, Father," sang Juliet, dashing past Friar Lawrence and leaping into Romeo's arms.

"Juliet!" cried Romeo, holding her. "If your joy is as great as mine, sweeten this air with your breath. Tell me how happy you are to be here, how happy you will be once we are married."

"I cannot sum up my love with words," she said, and kissed him.

Romeo held her tightly in his arms, kissing her again and again.

"Come, come," said Friar Lawrence, separating the two. "We will make short work of this. Obviously, you cannot be left alone until the church incorporates you two in one."

Friar Lawrence led them to the altar and hastily administered the ceremony.

When he was through, he left them alone to pray in separate rooms. He went to his garden to think.

The nurse found him there. "The young man isn't welcome in his new wife's house," she said, "nor she in his. What are they supposed to do now? Where are they supposed to go?"

Friar Lawrence hadn't thought that far ahead. "In time, perhaps they will tell their parents."

"Father," the nurse smiled. "They are newlyweds. They will want to be together."

Friar Lawrence took his scissors from his pouch and began to snip at his vines. "The Lord provides." It was the best answer he had.

The nurse shrugged. "How?"

"I can't speak for Him," said Friar Lawrence, moving away.

"Aren't you supposed to?" asked the nurse.

"Well, what's your solution, then?" Friar Lawrence snapped, throwing his scissors to the ground. "You're as much to blame as I am. You helped get Juliet into this mess, you who are more of a parent to her than either of her parents. What would you have them do?"

"Father, you married them," she said. "You married them before God. If you thought you were to blame for doing so, you never should have done it!"

"So it's all my fault?"

"If you think it was wrong, yes!"

The two stared at each other for a long while. Friar Lawrence finally broke the silence. "They need our help, don't they?"

"All we can give and more," said the nurse. "And we need each other's help, too. Their parents will hang us from the city gates if they find out about this. We have to keep things quiet for a while, and that means we have to make sure those two have some time together to be man and wife. They'll settle down after that."

"Right," Friar Lawrence said. "Take the lady home. I will help Romeo devise some way into her chamber tonight. That should solve the immediate problem. We'll worry about their parents later."

Chapter Eleven

Benvolio frowned as a messenger whispered in his ear.

"Thanks," he said, giving the young man a coin and sending him on his way. "The Capulets are out," he said to Mercutio, "in force. They're looking for Romeo. Tybalt is furious. I think we should go."

"I'll not go," said Mercutio.

"I don't want to get dragged into a fight," insisted Benvolio. "Besides, we've been sitting here all day, and it's getting hot."

"Come, come," Mercutio replied. "Men who like fighting like the heat, and you like fighting as much as any man in Italy."

"Not me."

"Why, you'd quarrel with a man for coughing in the street and waking up your dog."

"You are such a man, Mercutio. Not I."

Mercutio scratched his chin. "Ah, yes," he said. "I must have been talking about myself."

"You always are."

Just then, Benvolio saw Tybalt and some of his friends making their way across the square.

"By my head," said Benvolio, "here come the Capulets. Let's go!"

"I don't care about them," said Mercutio.

"All the more reason to go. We don't want a fight."

But it was too late.

"Good afternoon," said Tybalt. "A word with one of you."

"A word?" Mercutio said. "'A word' is a strange word for a fight."

"You shall find me ready enough for fighting, sir," said Tybalt, setting a gloved hand on the hilt of his rapier, "if you will give me reason."

"Why can you only give when something has been given you first?" Mercutio jeered. "You are not very generous."

Tybalt stepped closer. "Mercutio, Romeo was with you last night, right? Where is he now?"

"Do you take me for his manservant?" asked Mercutio. "Do you think I am only here to give news of Romeo to the likes of you? Ha! If I knew where Romeo was I wouldn't tell you unless I knew for certain he were in hell, in which case I would urge you to go look for him there yourself."

Tybalt drew his sword.

"Gentlemen," interrupted Benvolio. "Either stop this quarrel or take it where you will not be seen. All eyes are on us here."

"No need," said Tybalt, as he saw Romeo coming toward them. "Here comes my man."

"Your man?" said Mercutio, taunting Tybalt. "How you like to speak about your betters as if they were your servants. Your man!"

"A mistake," said Tybalt, as Romeo came up beside Mercutio. "'Man' is too good. 'Villain' suits him better." He turned to Romeo. "And you are a villain."

Romeo just smiled. "Tybalt," he said, "my love for you excuses your rage. I am no villain. In time you will learn that. Until then, farewell."

Tybalt took Romeo's reply for mockery. "These idle words do not excuse the injuries you have inflicted on my household, ruining our party last night with your insulting presence. Now, turn and draw!" Tybalt's sword sliced through the air with an ominous hiss.

"I've never injured you, Tybalt, nor could I now. I love you like a brother—more like a brother than you can imagine. The name Capulet I hold as dear as my own." He bowed. "Be satisfied."

Mercutio looked at Romeo. "What kind of vile, dishonorable submission is this?"

"I'd call it calm reason," said Benvolio. "Let's go our ways peacefully and be content."

"I'll be content when Tybalt has made his way to hell!" said Mercutio.

Tybalt lifted his blade. "I am ready for you, sir."

"Tybalt! Gentle Mercutio," said Romeo. "Put away your swords."

Mercutio pushed Romeo aside. "Now, rat-catcher," he snarled at Tybalt, "Let's see if your sword is as sharp as mine!"

Mercutio lunged. Tybalt deftly stepped aside and unleashed a storm of blows, each of which drove Mercutio further back toward the low wall below the fountain. Mercutio cursed him as their swords clashed.

"Tybalt! Mercutio! The prince has forbidden this! Stop! Benvolio—" Romeo shouted, "help me—come between them!"

Romeo leaped into the middle of the fight, throwing his arms around Mercutio, but Tybalt would not relent.

Mercutio tried to lift his sword to fend off Tybalt's final thrust, but Romeo held him fast.

The blade of Tybalt's sword plunged into Mercutio's chest.

"Ahhhh!" Mercutio cried, falling to the ground.

Tybalt withdrew his sword and wiped the blood off with a handkerchief, dropping it at Romeo's feet before fleeing with his friends.

Benvolio rushed to Mercutio. "How bad is it?"

"A scratch," Mercutio coughed, "but it's enough." He put his hand over the wound on his chest. The blood gushed through his fingers. "A plague!" he roared. "A plague on both your houses!"

"Courage," said Romeo. "The hurt cannot be much."

"No," said Mercutio, his senses leaving him. "It's not so deep as a well nor so wide as a church door, but it's enough. It will do." Blood began to trickle from the corners of his mouth. "A plague on both your houses," he wheezed. "Why the devil did you come between us, Romeo? I couldn't see his blade. I couldn't defend myself against it."

Romeo looked into his friend's eyes. They were starting to glaze over. "I was trying to stop you."

"You stopped me, all right. A plague on both your houses," Mercutio gasped, his voice failing. "They have made worms' meat of me."

"I'll take him to a surgeon," said Benvolio. He put his hand under Mercutio's neck and prepared to lift him, but as he did, he felt the feeble pulse fade away. He laid him back down. "Dead," he said. "Romeo, brave Mercutio is dead."

Romeo stared at the bloody handkerchief Tybalt had dropped in the dust. This gallant man, the prince's kinsman and my friend, received this mortal wound on my behalf as I held him back, he thought. And Tybalt mocks me. Mocks us all. Oh, Juliet, if I could have married you but one day later, Tybalt would not be my cousin, and I could make him answer for this crime. Rage began to burn inside Romeo, burn away all the love and tenderness that had, only moments before, been all he could feel. In an instant he forgot about Juliet, about his marriage, about the future. He wanted justice and vengeance now, and he wanted blood.

He picked up Mercutio's sword.

"Romeo," said Benvolio, "put that blade away. Here comes Tybalt back again."

But Romeo did not put the sword down. "So, you've returned to see Mercutio slain and us groveling at the feet of a murderer. No. No, Tybalt!" he yelled. "Take your insults back—or keep them with you when I send you to keep Mercutio company."

Tybalt swaggered up to Romeo. "You wretched little boy," he said, "you consorted with him in life and will follow him in death."

"This sword and not your boasts will determine that," Romeo said, and struck.

Tybalt parried Romeo's blow with graceful ease, but Romeo pressed on like a fury. Tybalt tried to keep his composure, tried to make it seem as if he were toying with an inferior opponent, but it soon became clear that he was fighting not with a man but with an avenging angel.

Romeo slashed at Tybalt so violently that he could no longer feel his arm nor the sword he gripped in his hands. Beyond the flash of the blades, the cruel eyes of Tybalt simmered in Romeo's soul. He reached down deep for cruelty of his own, raining powerful blows on Tybalt. As he did, he saw the eyes of his enemy turn from smug confidence to exhaustion to panic and then to horror.

Suddenly there was no more ringing of swords, no more shouting. The vicious, handsome face of Tybalt became serene, and it was only then that Romeo saw how much he looked like Juliet. He watched Tybalt's body fall to the ground.

"Away! Be gone!" yelled Benvolio. "Tybalt's dead. The prince will doom you to death if you are found here."

Romeo dropped his sword. It was covered with the blood of Tybalt, the blood of his dear wife's dearest kinsman. "Oh, I am fortune's fool," he said.

"They are coming!" Benvolio screamed. "Romeo, get out of here!"

Chapter Twelve

Juliet stood on her balcony, watching the sun make its slow way down the western sky.

"Run, run, horses of the sky," she chanted. "Pull the sun downward into cloudy midnight. Spread your dark curtain so that Romeo may leap to these arms unheard and unseen."

She held out her arms and imagined closing them around Romeo. Romeo . . . she could almost feel him in the sound of his name.

"Come," she said, closing her arms around her body. "Come, gentle night; come, loving black-browed night. Give me my Romeo; and when he shall die, take him and cut him out in little stars, and he will make the face of heaven so fine that all the world will be in love with night, and pay no worship to the garish sun."

The nurse slipped through the curtain and out onto the balcony. Her face was ashen.

Juliet knew something was wrong. "Why do you look like that?"

"He's dead," she said.

The words hit Juliet like cold wind. "Are the gods so jealous of my love? My Romeo? My love? Dead?"

"No," said the nurse, but the truth was little better. "No. Tybalt. Tybalt is dead. Slain by Romeo. And Romeo has been banished by the prince."

"Did . . . Romeo's hand shed Tybalt's blood?" Juliet could barely speak as the tears welled up in her eyes.

"There is no faith, no honesty in men," lamented the nurse. "Shame come to Romeo!"

Juliet flew into a sudden fit. "May your tongue be blistered for uttering such a wish!"

"Will you speak well of him that killed your cousin?"

"Shall I speak ill of him that is my husband? My cousin would have killed Romeo, who happily is living still." She choked back her sobs. "So why can I not stop weeping? I should be glad. Romeo is not dead and only banished."

The tears came again. "Banished! That one word kills a thousand Tybalts. He shall never come again to Verona nor to me. Banished! Oh, my wedding bed shall be my deathbed. Banished!"

As angry as she was at Romeo for killing Tybalt, the nurse forgave him that instant out of tenderness for the young woman whose life and happiness were her greatest cares. And Tybalt, she knew, was no angel. She stroked Juliet's hair and patted her cheek. "Go into your chamber, dear lady," she said. "I'll find your husband yet."

Romeo stepped forth from the shadows when Friar Lawrence returned to his cell. "Well, Father? What news? What is the prince's judgment?"

Friar Lawrence removed his travelling cloak and hung it on a peg next to his gardening apron. "A gentle judgment," he said, knowing full well that Romeo would think otherwise. "Not death, but banishment."

"Banishment!" Romeo wailed. "Be merciful and say 'death,' for exile is worse than death."

"Be patient," said Friar Lawrence smiling, "the world is broad and wide."

"There is no world outside Verona's walls!"

"You don't know what you're saying."

"I know I'd sooner die here than live banished!"

Friar Lawrence knew that Romeo was speaking out of passion, but still the words rankled him. "Ingratitude is a deadly sin, my boy," he said. "The prince could have called for your head—or your father's or your father-in-law's. He didn't. He listened to your mother's entreaty. She argued that, according to law, Tybalt should have died for murdering Mercutio, and that you were only doing what the law would have done anyway. The prince is acting mercifully with you. Can't you see that?"

"It is torture and not mercy!" cried Romeo. "Heaven is here where Juliet lives, and every cat and dog and unworthy thing here may look on her, but I may not. And yet you say that exile is not death? Can't you see that life without her is death?"

"I see that madmen have no ears," said Friar Lawrence.

There was a frantic knocking at the door.

"Hide yourself, Romeo," said Friar Lawrence.

Romeo did not move.

"Coming," yelled Friar Lawrence. "Romeo," he whispered, "there is a world remaining still, have faith in that. Now conceal yourself or be arrested."

Romeo slumped back into the shadows. Friar Lawrence opened the door.

It was the nurse. "Good afternoon, Friar," she said. "Is Romeo here?"

"Drunk on his own tears, but here," he said. "Romeo!"

He came forward.

"He looks like my lady," said the nurse. "All tears and howling."

"You break my heart, nurse," said Romeo, "to speak of her tears."

"And you break hers," she said. "She calls for Tybalt and calls for you, but nobody comes."

"Because the same villain that murdered her cousin has left her to suffer alone," said Romeo. "And I will be Juliet's champion yet and kill that villain." He drew his dagger and placed the tip against his chest.

"Don't you do that!" Friar Lawrence slapped the dagger to the floor. "Are you a man? You look like one, but your wild act denotes the unreasonable fury of a beast. You amaze me, you really do. You've murdered Tybalt—a mistake. But will you kill yourself and in so doing murder the young lady, too? Was it only the passion of the moment that made you profess love and faith to her?

She lives still. Will you abandon her by taking your own life? The prince has given you a chance to live. Can't you calm yourself and think of how you may make use of that chance?"

Romeo collapsed in a chair.

Friar Lawrence collected himself and put his hand on Romeo's head. "Go to your love. Ascend to her chamber as we planned. Comfort her. When you have done this, we'll get you out of the city. In Mantua, you will live until we have found some way to patch things up between your families. If your love is strong enough, it will endure."

"Good counsel," said the nurse. "I'll go to my lady and tell her you will come."

"And I will find your man," said Friar Lawrence. "He'll make ready for your journey. But go to Juliet now. She needs you. She needs you to be strong."

Chapter Thirteen

Capulet stood behind his writing table wearing armor he had not put on in many years. Paris stood by quietly and obediently, like a spaniel waiting for a stick to be thrown.

Capulet's knees ached and he wanted to sit down, but he didn't let himself. With Tybalt's death, he realized that he had grown soft in his old age, that he had given the young ones too much rein. Tybalt hadn't listened to him and so he had died. Capulet wasn't going to allow his only daughter to make the same mistake. "Wife," he commanded, "speak to Juliet before you go to bed. Tell her of . . . of Paris' love and bid her—do you hear me?—bid her that on Wednesday next . . . Wait. What day is this?"

"Monday, my lord," said Paris.

"Wednesday is too soon. Thursday, then. Tell her that on Thursday she will be married."

Lady Capulet bowed and left.

"Does this suit you?" Capulet asked Paris.

"I only wish Thursday were tomorrow," he answered.

Upstairs, in Juliet's bedroom, Romeo placed a final kiss on his lover's lips.

"Must you leave so soon?" Juliet said.

"I must be gone and live, or stay and die."

"Stay and let us die together," she said, folding her arms around Romeo's shoulders as he buckled his shoes.

He turned and kissed her. "I will if you will."

"My lady!" whispered the nurse, pushing open the bedroom door. "Your mother is coming."

"Then it is farewell, my wife and my love," said Romeo. "One kiss and I'll descend."

He stroked the hair away from her face and kissed her forehead.

"My love, my lord, my husband, and my friend," Juliet said. "I must hear from you every day."

"Farewell," he said again. "I will write every chance I get."

"When do you think we will meet again?"

"Soon. . ."

"Hurry!" cried the nurse. "She's on the stair!"

"I'm frightened," said Juliet.

"Trust me, love," Romeo said.

He kissed away a tear that rolled slowly down Juliet's cheek, stepped out onto the balcony, and climbed down the trellis.

"How are you, Juliet?" Lady Capulet said, pushing the door open.

"Madam, I am not well," said Juliet, dressing quickly.

"Still weeping for your cousin's death?" Lady Capulet entered the room. "We are all sorry for it."

She went to the window and saw the sunrise glowing sickly and pink at the bottom of the deep, soothing night. "But you weep not for his death so much as for the villain who slaughtered him."

Juliet froze. Had she been discovered? "What villain do you mean, madam?"

"That villain Romeo," she said. "Your worthy cousin is dead and yet the villain lives. It is for that you weep."

"Yes," Juliet said, relieved. "Yes. I wish I could get my hands on that Romeo."

"Leave that to me," her mother returned. "I will send a man to Mantua who will give Romeo what he deserves."

"I would go myself," said Juliet.

Her mother seemed not to hear. "You have other business. Next Thursday morning the noble gentleman Paris will make you a joyful bride at Saint Peter's Church."

"No, he shall not!" Juliet exclaimed, before she had time to think about what she was saying.

Lady Capulet scowled, though she did not seem surprised. "You disobey?"

"I mean," Juliet said, trying to placate her mother, "it isn't possible."

"Then you disobey."

Slow footsteps scraped on the stairs outside the bedroom. "Here comes your father. Tell him so yourself."

Capulet lumbered into the bedroom. "Well, have you delivered our decree?"

"I have," Lady Capulet said, "but she will have none of it. She doesn't appreciate how good it will be to have as her companion a handsome young husband. Let the fool marry her grave, and see if she likes that any better."

"Father," Juliet said, "I cannot marry Paris."

"But it is my wish for you," Capulet said.

"I thank you for your wishes, but I cannot."

"Do my wishes mean nothing to you?"

"As much as my own, but I am powerless to grant those, too."

"What is this cunning impudence?" bellowed Capulet. "Am I the master here or you? You go with Paris to Saint Peter's Church Thursday next or I will drag you there."

"I beseech you, father!" cried Juliet, falling and grasping her father's ankles. "You've always let me make decisions for myself. Hear mine now with patience."

"Decisions, disobedient wretch? I'll give you a decision to make. Get to that church next Thursday or never look me in the face again. Speak not, reply not, and answer not. Wife," he said, "it once seemed to us a sad thing that God only blessed us with one child, but now I see that one child was one too many."

"God in heaven," objected the nurse, "you are to blame for saying so!"

"Hold your tongue, you meddling fool!" Capulet stormed out of the room.

"Is there no pity for me?" pleaded Juliet. "Mother, do not cast me away. Delay this marriage for a month, a week; or, if you do not, make my bridal bed in the tomb where Tybalt lies."

"You should be so lucky as to lie with Tybalt," Lady Capulet snapped. "If your father casts you out of this house, you'll die in a ditch and lie there forever!"

Juliet sobbed and clutched at her mother.

Lady Capulet pushed her away. "Your father is trying to do what's best for you and for all of us. Talk no more to me, for I'll not speak a word. Do as you will, for I have done with you!"

She left Juliet alone with the nurse.

"How shall this crime be prevented? Say something! What shall I do?"

The nurse had no answer ready. If a lady's father casts her out and she has no husband who can take her in, then that lady starves. That is the way the world works. Then again, a vow made before God is a vow made before God. But God doesn't exactly put food on the table or keep the house warm at night.

"Nurse?" pleaded Juliet.

"All right," she said, "here is my advice." What to say?

"Here it is then." She sighed. "All right. Romeo's banished and can never come back. He alone knows you're married. Well, I know . . . and Friar Lawrence knows, but we'll keep quiet. See what I'm getting at? If you marry Paris, only Romeo can challenge the marriage, and he won't because he'll never set foot inside Verona."

Juliet was shocked. "Do you mean what I think you mean?"

"It's the only way," she said. "Why, Paris will make a lovely husband. He's the prince's kinsman! Romeo's a dishcloth beside him."

"A dishcloth?" said Juliet. She looked deeply into the nurse's eyes and saw something she had never seen there before. Uncertainty. More than that—fear. "You want me to marry Paris and forget all about my marriage to Romeo?"

"I . . . " the nurse stuttered. "Well . . . try to understand."

"I see," said Juliet.

"You'll be happier," the nurse returned, mustering confidence for Juliet's sake, if not for her own.

"I see," repeated Juliet.

"Paris is a fine man," the nurse went on. "Before you know it, you'll—"

"Thank you, nurse," said Juliet stiffly. "You need not say anything more. I am convinced. Go tell my mother and father that I will do their bidding."

The nurse felt her stomach turn as she watched Juliet march to the door and hold it open. This girl—this woman—who was like her own daughter had come to her for help and all she could do was lie. What was worse, Juliet knew she had lied. Romeo was a better man than Paris any day of the week, and, more important, Juliet was already his wife! The nurse fought back tears. Please, she thought, please understand and forgive me someday.

"I said I am convinced, nurse," said Juliet, crossing her arms. "So you may go. In the morning I will go to Friar Lawrence's cell to confess the sin of disobedience."

"That's wisely done," said the nurse. "May I . . . go with you to the friar's in the morning?"

"No," said Juliet. "You've helped enough already."

Chapter Fourteen

"Thursday is too soon," said Friar Lawrence, scratching at a row of asparagus with his hoe.

"It is her father's decree," said Paris.

"But what does Juliet say?"

"She has been too distraught with her cousin's death to think much about love," Paris explained sheepishly. "But her father assures me she will marry me. His course is set."

"Hasn't her father's stubbornness caused enough trouble in her life?"

"Sir?"

Friar Lawrence stopped hoeing. He shouldn't have said that. Paris wasn't one to question anyone or anything, especially not men with the power and importance of old Capulet. "I'm sorry," he said, "but such haste—and you don't know the lady's mind? I don't like it."

"I grant," said Paris diplomatically, "there are reasons to think this marriage may be starting off inauspiciously, but her father has given his consent and proclaimed that the ceremony should be Thursday. There is no reason in heaven or on earth why it shouldn't."

Friar Lawrence took a deep breath and looked up at the sky. God, he said to himself, if you will make me a braver man, I will put an end to this trouble now.

"What say the heavens?" asked Paris.

"Friar Lawrence!" came a voice.

Friar Lawrence looked down the path and saw Juliet winding her way through his vines and fruit trees, her head covered in a black mourning hood.

"Oh, she will someday run to me like that and call my name," Paris said.

Friar Lawrence ignored him. "What is it, my daughter?"

She froze when she saw Paris. "Nothing, Father," she said. "Only, I have come to make confession."

"Hello, Juliet." Paris bowed.

Juliet curtseyed mechanically and sent a despairing look at Friar Lawrence.

"Good Paris," he said, "you must give us this time alone."

"Of course," he said. "Juliet, I will rouse you on Thursday. Until then, adieu. But keep this holy kiss."

Juliet pulled her hand away before Paris' lips could touch it. Paris seemed unperturbed. He waved goodbye and stepped happily down the path.

"Oh, Juliet," said Friar Lawrence, once Paris was out of earshot. "I hear you must on Thursday next be married to Paris."

Juliet looked at him quizzically. "Don't tell me, Friar, that you heard of this unless you will also tell me that you will prevent it."

Friar Lawrence put aside his hoe and lifted his arms. "Please understand . . ."

"I see how it is," said Juliet. "First my nurse and now you. You joined Romeo and me, and yet you will not step in to prevent this second, unlawful marriage." She stormed away but stopped short and turned. "You amaze me, you older people. You are all full of courage and truth when there is nothing to fear, but when trouble comes you hide your heads. Is this the wisdom I can expect to gain as the years go by? To start what one does not intend to finish? To run away from problems? To sell out one's beliefs to save one's skin? And to leave the young people all alone to suffer the consequences for one's decisions? Well, I was prepared for this!" She pulled a dagger from the folds of her robe.

"Juliet!" exclaimed Friar Lawrence, "what are you doing?"

She put the tip of the dagger against her heart. "Since you have no wisdom to share, I will trust my own wisdom. This bloody knife will put to rest a problem that you will not help resolve."

"Hold, my daughter!" cried Friar Lawrence. "There is hope."

"In what?"

Friar Lawrence thought quickly. His eyes fell on the dark purple blossoms behind Juliet, and he had an idea. "Here," he said, plucking the flowers. "Extracts from these blooms induce a death-like sleep. Come with me. I will prepare a vial for you. When you are home, secure yourself in your chamber and drink it down. You will feel a cold and drowsy humor overcome you—even your pulse will stop. Later, when they take your body to your family vault, I will retrieve you. By letter I'll tell Romeo of the plan—and he shall come too! Have no fear."

A wild and determined look came over Juliet's face. "Give it to me! I'm not afraid."

Friar Lawrence hurried into his kitchen to make the medicine. Juliet sat at the table as fixed and resolute as a statue. That's courage, Friar Lawrence thought as he crushed the purple blossoms into the bottom of the pestle. If only there were an herb or a flower that could give a tired old fool that kind of nerve!

Chapter Fifteen

The nurse laid out Juliet's wedding dress on her bed. "You'll be a pretty bride," she said. "A very pretty bride. Paris is a lucky man, indeed. I only wish it were morning now."

Capulet and his wife stood proudly by. "That Friar Lawrence is a good man," Capulet said in a low voice.

Juliet heard. "I must beg your pardon again," she said. "I have learned to repent the sin of disobedient opposition. Henceforward I am ever ruled by you, my noble father and mother." She gave a half smile and bowed.

"You are a perfect lady," said Capulet. "I won't pretend I won't miss the daughter I had, even to get so worthy a son as Paris."

Juliet moved the wedding dress and sat on the bed. "And now I beg you all to leave me to myself tonight, for I must continue to pray. As you know, I have lately been cross and full of sin."

"That's behind you now, my lady," protested the nurse.

"Come, come, leave her to pray," said Capulet. "Daughter, you have made me very happy." He hobbled out of the bedroom.

"Shall I wait by you tonight?" the nurse asked in a whisper.

"Thank you," Juliet did not so much as look at the nurse, "but I fear to ask anything more of you."

The words cut to the bone. "I would do anything for you, you know that," the nurse said softly.

"Then leave me," Juliet said.

The nurse trudged out of the room.

"So we are alone, daughter," said Lady Capulet, closing the door after the nurse. "Do you want some words of advice from me? I was once a young girl about to be married."

"If you would just keep the nurse from me, madam," Juliet answered. "Since this marriage is so sudden, I'm sure there are many details of the feast yet to be attended to. I would not want to keep you from that important and sudden business."

Lady Capulet supposed there was an insult there, but she let it pass—almost. "You will be happier once you are made a wife and a mother and have a house of you own. Most girls are."

"Aye, madam. I will be as happy as you will be once I am married and out of the house. Now please leave me to pray that I might be as good a wife and mother as your gracious self."

"Get some sleep," said Lady Capulet coldly. "You will need it."

She left.

Juliet silently closed the door and withdrew from her bag the vial of potion Friar Lawrence had given her. She held it to the light and studied the swirling blue powder suspended in the liquid.

It occurred to her that the potion Friar Lawrence prepared might be a real poison. He might, after all, want to kill her in order to prevent her secret marriage from being discovered. No, she thought, Friar Lawrence was afraid—that much was certain—but he had always been a friend. He would not murder her. She shook the bottle. And even if, in his desperation, he had become a murderer, she decided, there was no other solution left but to go through with the plan, whatever might happen.

She took a deep breath and uncorked the bottle.

But another fear gripped her.

What if she were to wake up before Romeo
came? Would she not then suffocate in
the vault? Worse, what if, surrounded in
the dark tomb with so many horrible
images of death, she lost her mind?
What if, waking up beside Tybalt,
moldering in his bloody shroud, she
succumbed to madness and dashed
out her brains with the bones of
one of her deceased kinsmen?
What if . . .

"Enough of 'what ifs,'" she
whispered. "Here is the only
answer." She put the bottle
to her lips. "Romeo, I
come!" She poured the
potion down her
throat. "This do I
drink to thee."

Her throat
burned. She
gagged.
Bright lights
appeared
before her
eyes. Her hands
went numb and
then her legs. She felt
herself falling.

And then nothing.

In the hours just before dawn, the nurse rose from the drawing room.

"One word of courage," she mumbled. "That's all. She can't begrudge me one word of courage on the night before her wedding."

She waddled up the stairs and slid open Juliet's door. On tiptoe she went to where her young lady lay sleeping. She put a hand on her cold forehead.

Her scream woke the entire house.

Chapter Sixteen

Balthasar's hand shook as he opened the door of Romeo's apartment in Mantua.

"Ah," Romeo said, "news from Verona. Do you bring me letters from the friar? How does my lady? Is my father well? How is my Juliet? I'll ask again, for nothing can be bad if she is well."

"Then she is well and nothing can be bad," answered Balthasar. "Her immortal part lives with the angels. We should all be so fortunate."

"Her soul has always dwelt with angels," Romeo beamed, "but what about the rest of her?"

"My lord, I . . ." He couldn't bring himself to say it. "Her body . . . sleeps in the Capulets' tomb."

Romeo rose slowly from his desk. "What do you mean?"

"I . . . saw her laid low in the vault. She . . . she is dead."

"Can it be?"

"I wish it were not."

Romeo laughed bitterly. "The stars have always been jealous that one so perfect dared to live beneath them." He trembled and clenched his fists. Then he pounded them on the desk. He kicked the chair across the room where it broke into splinters against the wall.

"Then I defy you, stars!" he roared. "Go, Balthasar. Get me horses. Meet me by the city walls. I will leave tonight."

"I beseech you, sir," said Balthasar, "calm your passions. Nothing good can come of this rage."

Romeo gathered his things and hastily packed them into a bag. "You are deceived. What you see is not rage." He struggled to control his voice. "It is a reasonable response to a gross, horrible, hateful injustice! Now, go and do what I told you."

"Sir . . ."

"Go!"

Balthasar left.

"Juliet," said Romeo, "I will lie with thee tonight."

But how, he wondered.

Then he remembered. There was in Mantua an apothecary who dealt in strange drugs. Meager were his looks; misery had worn him to the bone, and in his shop a tortoise hung, an alligator stuffed, and other skins of ill-shaped fishes. It was said that for a price he would sell the means by which a man might end his own life, or that of another. Romeo shook some gold from his purse and counted it. The price for such drugs would be high, but he had enough.

He threw his bag over his shoulder, tucked his dagger into his belt, and strode out.

No sooner had he disappeared down the alleyway when a monk in a dusty brown tunic arrived at Romeo's apartment.

"Hello!" he cried. "I have a letter for Romeo! Hello?" He rapped at the window. "It comes from Friar Lawrence, and I am told it is of great importance! Is anyone there? Hello?"

No one was there to answer.

Chapter Seventeen

Friar Lawrence stayed close to the trees by the side of the road as he made his way to the churchyard where Juliet lay sleeping in her family crypt. By the height of the moon he could tell that it was almost midnight, which meant that the potion would soon wear off and Juliet would awaken. He shuddered to think about what it would be like to wake up in a cold charnel house surrounded by dead bones. Such courage she has, he thought.

He picked up his pace until he arrived at the crossroads where he had instructed Romeo to meet him.

There was nobody there.

He waited for what seemed like an eternity.

Finally, from down the road came the figure of a man. It didn't look like Romeo, but who else would be heading to the graveyard at this time of night?

"Who's there?" called Friar Lawrence.

"Brother? Friar Lawrence?" returned the voice. "Is that you?"

"Friar John?" asked Friar Lawrence, squinting into the darkness.

"Bless me, yes," said Friar John. "What good luck meeting you here."

"What are you doing here?" asked Friar Lawrence. "Where is Romeo?"

"That's what I came to talk about. I had quite an ordeal in Mantua. Hooo!"

"Did you bring the letter to Romeo?"

"Never got the chance," said Friar John, casually. "I was quarantined at the customs house. I guess some other Franciscan friars had carried plague into the city at Bologna, and the Mantuan officials were taking extra precautions. By the time they let me in, Romeo was gone. Anyway, here's the letter back. Nice night, isn't it?"

"Unhappy fortune," Friar Lawrence intoned. "No doubt he's heard of Juliet's death by now and has . . . has . . . dear God, what has he done?"

"You seem distressed, my brother."

"Go to my lodging," Friar Lawrence said. "Wait there in case Romeo shows up. Tell him Juliet is alive."

Friar John did not quite understand, but he did as he was told.

Now I must go to the tomb alone, thought Friar Lawrence.

And he shuddered again.

Chapter Eighteen

"Wait here with the torch, boy," said Paris to his servant.

"I . . . I am afraid to stand alone here in the graveyard, sir."

"Then stand off by the road, and whistle if you see any ghosts."

Paris' servant stepped on timid feet through the gravestones.

Paris went to the tomb of the Capulets. There he knelt at the iron door and dropped flower petals. This, he told himself, I will do every night as a symbol of my eternal devotion to Juliet— so that everyone will know how much I loved her.

As he scattered the petals, he heard his servant whistle. Was it a ghost? Paris looked across the graveyard and saw a figure like a man approaching. He caught his breath and quickly hid himself behind a large stone near the tomb.

This is no ghost, he thought, as he saw the man come nearer, carrying a torch. This is Romeo! With a crowbar! The man who killed Tybalt, for whom my lady died grieving. And now he comes here to vandalize the tomb! Not while I'm here, he resolved. In this defense of my Juliet's resting place, I will further demonstrate my love!

Romeo set the crowbar to the door and began to pry it open.

"Stop your unholy work, vile Montague," Paris commanded, stepping forward. "Will you seek vengeance on the Capulets even in their grave? Condemned villain, by coming back here you are violating the prince's decree."

"Do not tempt me. I am desperate," Romeo said without lifting his eyes from his work. "Run away and leave me. Pray for those who have died, and, please, do not force me to commit another sin by killing you."

The door groaned open.

Paris grabbed Romeo by the arm. "I arrest you for a felon."

When Romeo felt the hand on his arm, he whirled and swung the crowbar into Paris' skull. Paris wheezed and fell to the earth. His servant, who had been watching, ran off to tell the soldiers.

"If . . . you are merciful . . . lay me beside Juliet," Paris sputtered as he died.

Beside Juliet? Romeo looked at what was left of the face of the man he had killed and recognized him. He was the one who had been dancing with Juliet at the Capulet's party.

He closed Paris' eyes.

"I forgive you," he said, "and I will lay you down beside her. It is not wrong to have been in love with Juliet, though you died for it, as I am about to."

He dragged Paris' body into the vault.

There on an alabaster slab, around which were scattered the dusty bones of all the Capulets who had come before, he found Juliet lying beneath a gossamer shroud.

Romeo fell to his knees. "Oh, my love, my wife," he said, "death has taken your life, but it has not touched your beauty." He lifted the gauze from her face. "Ah, dear Juliet, why are you still so fair?" He knew why, or at least he thought he did. Even the god of death wanted to keep her for his own, forever young and forever beautiful. Well, death, he said to himself, I hate to spoil your love affair with my wife, but I will stay here, too, watching over her—forever.

He brushed the hair back from Juliet's face. "Eyes," he said, "look your last. Arms, take your last embrace. And lips, the very doors of breath, seal with a righteous kiss." He pressed his lips against hers.

Then he opened a small bottle. The smell itself caused Romeo to recoil, but his course was set. "Here's to my love!" he said and tossed back the potion he had purchased from the apothecary in Mantua. His face contorted. His stomach heaved. "The drugs," he coughed, "are quick." He lowered his lips once more to Juliet's. "Thus, with a kiss, I die."

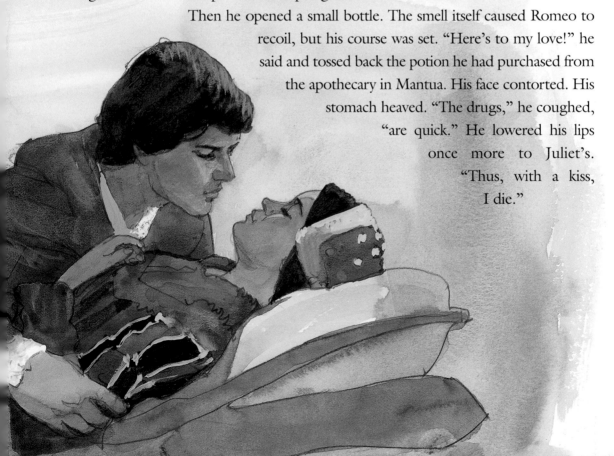

His body shuddered and became still.

"Who's in here?" called Friar Lawrence as he pushed his way into the vault, the bloody crowbar in his hand. He feared the worst. "Hello?"

He lifted his lantern and saw the mangled face of Paris. He turned away in horror, but as he did, he saw something even worse. Romeo—dead at the base of the monument where Juliet lay.

"Cruel fate," he muttered. "One hour earlier, and all could have been saved."

Juliet groaned.

"And now the lady stirs!"

Juliet raised herself upright and looked around disoriented. Then she saw Friar Lawrence.

"Friar," she said. "Where is my husband? Here I am, but where is Romeo?"

The faint sound of hoof beats came through the open door of the crypt. "I hear some noise," said Friar Lawrence. "Come away from this foul place of death."

"Where is Romeo?" demanded Juliet.

Distant voices now trickled in. "I dare not stay!" whimpered Friar Lawrence. "Romeo . . . Romeo lies there on the ground. A power greater than ourselves has ruined our plan. Your husband is dead—and Paris, too. Now come on!"

"You may go," she said, stooping to examine Romeo.

"My lady, I dare not stay!"

"Then go," Juliet said, "for I will not."

Friar Lawrence looked at Juliet. He crossed himself and scurried out.

What's this? thought Juliet. A bottle held in my true love's hand? Poison, I see. She held the bottle up to the torchlight. And you've drunk all and left me none. Then I will kiss your lips—hopefully some poison still hangs on them.

She kissed Romeo and tasted the bitter potion he had swallowed. But it was not enough.

"Ha. His lips are still warm." She tossed the bottle to the ground.

The door of the monument creaked and in swept the clamor of many voices.

"I see they will never leave us alone, my love." Juliet shook her head. "But I will be brief." She took the dagger from Romeo's belt. "Oh, happy dagger! This is your sheath," she said, and ran the blade through her heart. "There . . . rest," she stammered, "and let . . . me . . . die."

She fell on top of Romeo just as the prince rushed in. Montague followed, as did Capulet and his wife, guarded by soldiers.

"Now we will see why the peace of my city has been broken—again—with shouts of 'Romeo' and 'Juliet' and 'Paris' and 'murder'!" The prince looked sternly at the two old men. "I do not doubt that the hate you bear each other is once again to blame. Give us more light!"

More torches were brought in.

All looked in horror at the sight before them.

"Scour the area," ordered the prince. "Find the murderer."

"A dagger," murmured Capulet, stooping to Juliet. "Oh, wife, look how our daughter bleeds!"

"Oh, rude boy," cried Montague, kneeling beside Romeo, weeping, "to proceed before your father to the grave!"

"Where is your wife, Montague?" asked the prince.

"Dead," he simpered, "tonight—of grief over Romeo's exile." Then his sadness turned to rage. "Exile for dealing justly with the murderer Tybalt!"

"And was it Tybalt who killed Paris and plunged this dagger into my daughter's breast?" barked Lady Capulet, resting her hand on Tybalt's corpse. "If only he were alive to do so!"

"Silence!" demanded the prince. "We'll get to the bottom of this without any accusations from you two."

A captain entered and whispered into the prince's ear.

He nodded gravely. "All right, then," the prince said, "bring the suspicious party in."

The captain gave an order and two soldiers came forward, dragging in Friar Lawrence and throwing him to the ground.

Friar Lawrence raised his hands, pleading. "I know I look guilty, and though I am guilty before God, I am not guilty of these murders."

"Then say at once what you know of this—and why you ran away," said the prince.

Friar Lawrence told all. "Romeo, there dead, was husband to Juliet, and she, there dead, was Romeo's faithful wife. I married them."

Everyone gasped.

"Their wedding day was Tybalt's doomsday. It was for Romeo's banishment — not for Tybalt's death—that Juliet grieved." Friar Lawrence shook his head. "When you, old Capulet, promised her to Paris, she came to me and asked for some way to get out of the second marriage. And I—" Friar Lawrence saw the anger and disbelief simmer in the eyes of his audience. "I gave her a sleeping potion. She would have killed herself, there in my cell, if I hadn't, don't you see?"

"Tell on," said the prince.

"Romeo was to know about it. He was to come here tonight to retrieve her when she awoke, but my letter never reached him. When I came to take her to my cell, Romeo had already arrived, and, not knowing that his love lay sleeping and not dead, he took his own life." He looked at the body of Paris. "I assume Paris, your grace's kinsman, died attempting to stop Romeo from entering. I tried to keep Juliet from the sight of her dead lover, but I couldn't."

"Why didn't you stay with her?" asked Capulet weakly. "You knew what a fearless and headstrong girl she was. You knew what she would do if left alone."

"I . . . was . . . afraid. But . . . but I was not acting alone! Juliet's nurse—" He held his hands to his face and began to weep. "Oh, I am a coward," he sobbed. "I await your punishment."

"Enough," the prince said. "It's true that you who were supposed to shepherd these young people—supposed to show them what was right and proper—have acted cravenly and most injudiciously. But the guilt you will bear is punishment enough," he scowled at Friar Lawrence. "And though your fault is great, it is small compared to *yours*." He turned to Capulet and Montague. "See what has come of your ancient grudge? You've lost your only children, and I, by allowing your discord to go on for too long, have lost two members of my family—first Mercutio and now Paris."

Capulet looked up from the body of his daughter and saw his weary old enemy kneeling across from him. "Brother Montague," he said, "give me your hand. And take my hand as my daughter's dowry, for I have nothing left to give you."

Montague leaned across the bodies of Romeo and Juliet and put his arms around Capulet. "But I can give more. I will raise your daughter's statue in pure gold."

"And I will put one of Romeo by her side."

From outside the tomb came the lonely call of a dove. "A gloomy peace this morning with it brings. The sun for sorrow will not show his head." Prince Escalus lifted the two old men to their feet. "Let us leave this place to have more talk of sad things. Some shall be pardoned, and some punished." He led the grieving people out of the tomb. "For never was a story of more woe," he said, "than this of Juliet and her Romeo."

ROMEO & JULIET

Because Shakespeare's time was very different from our own, many things that happen in the plays he wrote seem confusing. Knowing what life was like back then helps to clear up some of this confusion. Here are the answers to questions *Romeo and Juliet* often raises. If you have any questions of your own, write to me in care of the publisher, and I will try to answer them.

Why does Juliet have a nurse with her all the time?

The "nurse" in *Romeo and Juliet* is not a healthcare provider like the nurses you are used to. Back then, it was customary for wealthy mothers to hire poorer mothers to nurse their babies for them and generally to perform all of the tasks required for taking care of an infant. Since nurses were second mothers to the babies in their care, they often became part of the household, though they were still basically servants.

Why is this play set in Italy and not England?

Around 1400, a period began in Italy that we now call the "Renaissance," which means "rebirth." The Renaissance was an explosion of creative activity in all spheres of art and literature that by 1500 had changed the way people in virtually every European country wrote, painted, sculpted, constructed buildings, and organized universities. In England, during Shakespeare's lifetime, the Renaissance was still very new and exciting. English people associated the ideas and styles of the Renaissance with Italy, where they began over a century earlier. By setting *Romeo and Juliet* in Italy, Shakespeare is proclaiming its participation in all that was considered fresh, stylish, and intellectually important.

Didn't Shakespeare write "A rose by any other name would smell as sweet" (page 36)?

Why in this book does Juliet say, "A rose by any other word. . ."? Part of the fun of reading Shakespeare is that we cannot say for sure what Shakespeare wrote, since he did not oversee the publication of any of his plays. Although some of Shakespeare's plays were printed during his lifetime, many of these editions contain errors. A good collection of Shakespeare's works was published shortly after he died, but even this edition is not completely reliable. For this reason, any Shakespeare play printed today is the work of a scholar trying to put together the most accurate text based on the different versions of the play available. The famous line about "a rose by any other name" appears in an edition that most scholars now believe to be highly unreliable; the more reliable versions say "a rose by any other word," and so most new editions of *Romeo and Juliet*—including this one—have it written that way.

Why doesn't anyone think it strange that Romeo, Benvolio, and Mercutio show up at a party wearing masks?

In Shakespeare's time, a mask was a more common piece of apparel than it is now, especially for wealthy women who wished to conceal their identity in public places where the eyes of the gawking public might be upon them. Indeed, women often wore masks into the theater where Shakespeare's plays were performed. It was also fashionable for young men to wear masks at parties in order to give themselves an aura of mystery that was considered very attractive at the time.

If Romeo is banished from Verona, why is it okay for him to go to Mantua, another city in Italy?

Italy was not really a country in Shakespeare's time. Although most of what is now Italy was joined by a common culture and language, it was broken up into independent city-states under the control of a prince, duke, or "doge." A city like Verona would have been surrounded by walls, and it would have been governed by its own laws and protected by its own army.

Isn't Juliet too young to be married?

Yes and no. Thirteen would have been on the low side of what could have been considered a marriageable age for ordinary women, but among the nobility (an elite ruling class supposed to be inherently superior to everyone else), children were often married very early in order to create expedient political alliances.

Why is Friar John quarantined at Mantua?

The bubonic plague, or "Black Death," was a disease that swept through Europe in the middle of the fourteenth century, killing one in every three people in just a few years. Although the bubonic plague returned from time to time over the next centuries, European people were no longer as susceptible to the disease as they once were. First of all, most people were descendants of those who had survived the first epidemic. Secondly, cities had learned ways of controlling the plague's catastrophic effects: quarantine was the most common way. Upon receiving news of a plague outbreak, a city would shut its gates (remember that cities back then were walled like fortresses) and no one would be allowed in until the outbreak died down. Another way of controlling the plague was to restrict public gatherings where, then as now, disease spreads more easily. The city of London, for example, closed the theaters several times during Shakespeare's career when plague outbreaks occurred.

WHO'S WHO IN
ROMEO & JULIET

ABRAHAM: a servant employed by the Montagues

BALTHASAR: a servant employed by the Montagues

BENVOLIO: Romeo's cousin

CAPULET ("OLD CAPULET"): a Veronese gentleman and Juliet's father

ESCALUS: Prince of Verona

FRIAR JOHN: a monk and friend of Friar Lawrence

FRIAR LAWRENCE: a monk residing in Verona

GREGORY: a servant employed by the Capulets

JULIET: a young gentlewoman of Verona and Old Capulet's daughter

LADY CAPULET: Juliet's mother

LADY MONTAGUE: Romeo's mother

MERCUTIO: Prince Escalus' kinsman and friend of the Montagues

MONTAGUE ("OLD MONTAGUE"): a Veronese gentleman and Romeo's father

NURSE: Juliet's personal servant and former wet nurse

PARIS: Prince Escalus' kinsman and suitor to Juliet

SAMPSON: a servant employed by the Capulets

TYBALT: Juliet's cousin

INDEX